IT'S NOT MY TRUTH, IT'S THE TRUTH

STANDING FOR TRUTH IN A CULTURE OF RELATIVISM

SCOTT FARLEY

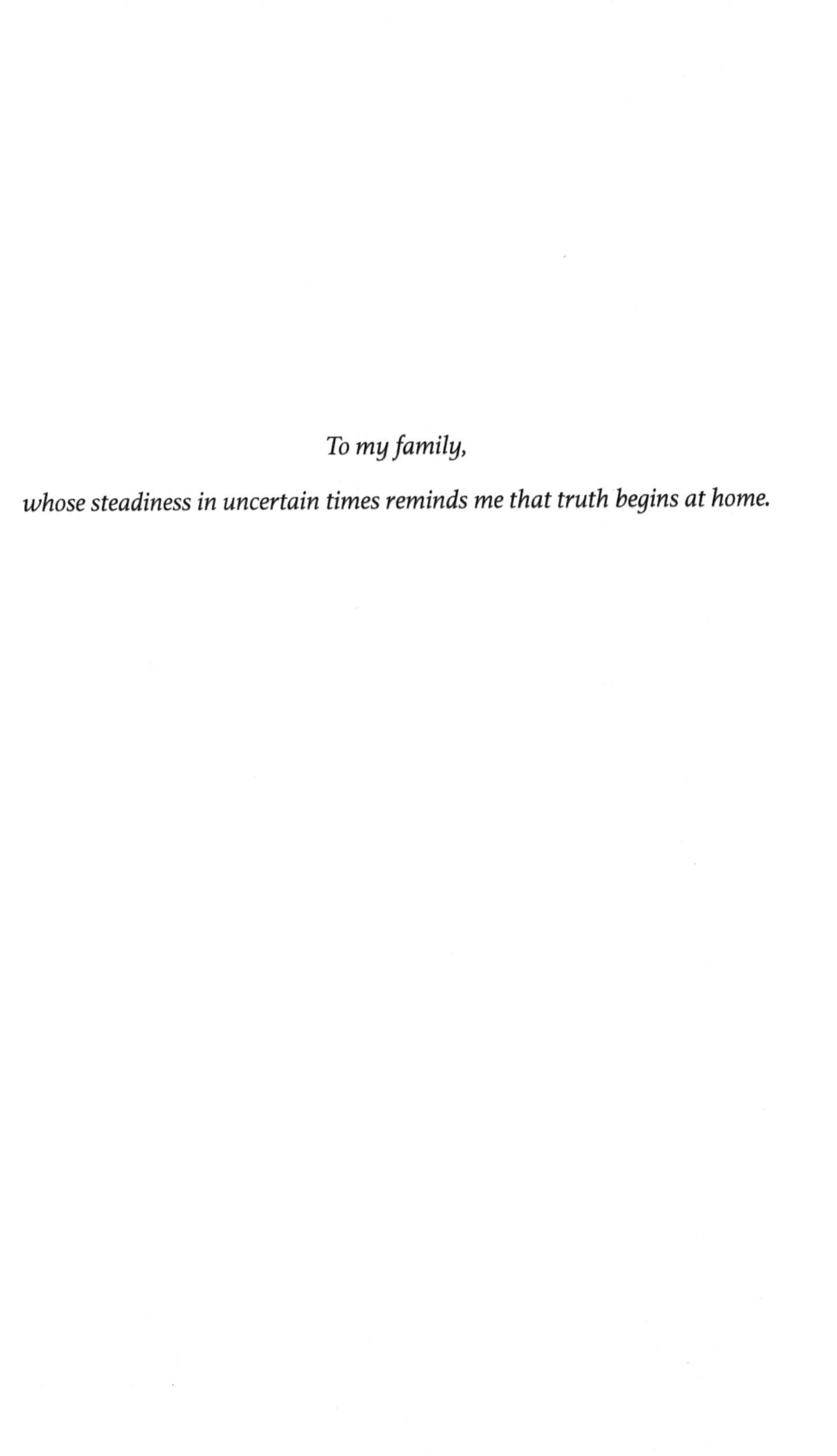

To my family,

whose steadiness in uncertain times reminds me that truth begins at home.

INTRODUCTION
WHEN TRUTH MOVES

In a packed school board meeting in Loudoun County, Virginia, a father stepped to the microphone and said something that would have sounded obvious a generation ago:

"Biology is not a feeling."

The room erupted.

Some applauded. Others shouted. Phones captured every second.

What happened next was not just a local dispute about school policy.

It was evidence of something much deeper.

The West no longer agrees on what truth is — or whether truth exists at all.

Something has shifted in the modern West.

Not merely laws.

Not merely language.

Not merely politics.

Something deeper.

Conversations that once seemed settled now feel unstable. Questions of identity, authority, and morality no longer assume shared foundations. Institutions that once operated with broad agreement now function from competing assumptions about reality itself. Public debates often feel less like disagreements over policy and more like clashes between incompatible worldviews.

The turbulence we see is not accidental. It is rooted in a philosophical relocation.

For centuries, Western civilization operated largely from the assumption that truth was discovered, not invented. It was grounded in reality beyond the self — in natural law, divine revelation, and objective moral order. Individuals could misunderstand truth, resist it, or distort it, but they did not define it.

In recent decades, that assumption has weakened.

Increasingly, authority is located within the individual. Identity is framed as self-constructed. Meaning is treated as personal rather than received. Moral claims are evaluated by authenticity rather than alignment with objective order. In this framework, truth becomes expressive rather than revealed.

This relocation has consequences.

When truth is internalized, disagreement feels personal rather than philosophical. When identity is self-declared, limits feel oppressive. When institutions adopt competing foundations, coherence erodes. Cultural tension intensifies not merely because people disagree, but because they are reasoning from different starting points.

The fracture is not primarily political. It is epistemological. It concerns where authority resides.

I write not as a professional pundit or career academic, but as a citizen, a husband and father, a Marine veteran, and a church elder who has watched these shifts unfold within institutions that shape everyday life. The questions explored in these pages are not abstract.

They affect classrooms, congregations, homes, and public discourse. They affect how the next generation understands reality itself.

This book does not argue that cultural change is new. Societies have always wrestled with competing visions of reality. Nor does it assume that every modern development is decline. Technological advancement, expanded communication, and greater access to information have produced undeniable benefits.

But progress without philosophical grounding is unstable.

If truth is self-defined, then it shifts with preference. If identity is untethered from design, it becomes fluid. If institutions no longer share foundational assumptions, trust weakens. Over time, fragmentation replaces coherence.

The result is not merely disagreement. It is disorientation.

Yet disorientation is not destiny.

History demonstrates that societies recalibrate. Ideas rise and recede. Philosophies that appear dominant may weaken under their own contradictions. Cultural confidence shifts as generations reassess inherited assumptions. The present moment, though turbulent, is not irreversible.

Recalibration begins with clarity.

If truth is not constructed but revealed — grounded in the character of God and embedded within creation — then it remains steady even when culture shifts. It does not require reinvention. It requires recognition.

The Christian claim has always affirmed that reality precedes preference. Human dignity is bestowed, not negotiated. Moral order is discovered, not declared. Freedom flourishes not in autonomy from design but in alignment with it.

When these convictions shape families, churches, and institutions, stability follows. When they are displaced, fragmentation accelerates.

This book seeks to examine that displacement.

It will explore the philosophical shift that relocated authority to the self. It will consider the cultural and institutional consequences of that shift. It will address how churches, families, educators, and leaders can respond not with panic or hostility, but with steadiness.

The goal is not dominance. It is coherence.

The goal is not cultural triumphalism. It is durable faithfulness.

The responsibility before this generation is not to invent a new moral order, nor to retreat from public life in frustration. It is to rebuild wisely — to inhabit institutions with integrity, to teach truth patiently, to lead without hysteria, and to cultivate endurance rather than spectacle.

Cultural turbulence often tempts reactive voices. But reaction rarely produces renewal. Renewal requires formation.

What follows is not a manifesto. It is an argument.

An argument that truth exists beyond preference.

An argument that institutions reflect their foundations.

An argument that stability depends on coherence.

And an argument that rebuilding is possible.

The moment is restless.

But restlessness is not permanent.

Where authority resides will determine what endures.

1

THE QUESTION
BENEATH THE CHAOS

In 2023 and 2024, school board meetings in Virginia, California, New Jersey, and Colorado drew national attention as parents, teachers, and activists debated gender identity policies in public schools. Districts including Fairfax County, Loudoun County, and Arlington in Virginia implemented or defended policies allowing students to use names and pronouns consistent with their gender identity. In some cases, district guidance stated that staff should not automatically disclose a student's gender identity to parents if such disclosure could pose a risk to the student's emotional well-being. Similar policies appeared in other states, prompting lawsuits, federal complaints, and heated public comment sessions streamed online.

These conflicts were not isolated to education. In recent years, major corporations updated workplace guidelines regarding pronoun usage and gender identity protections. Professional associations revised position statements. State legislatures passed laws either expanding gender identity protections or restricting medical transition procedures for minors. Federal agencies issued and revised interpretations of Title IX. The debates intensified through social media, where short clips of school board confrontations and legislative hearings reached millions within hours.

At first glance, these events appear to be political disputes. They involve policy language, civil rights statutes, and administrative authority. Yet beneath the legal arguments lies a more fundamental disagreement—one that predates modern politics and cannot be resolved through policy alone.

The disagreement concerns the nature of truth.

From Objective to Subjective Truth

For much of Western history, truth was understood as something objective—something that exists independent of individual perception. A person might misunderstand truth, deny it, or suppress it. But truth itself was assumed to exist outside the self. Scientific inquiry operated on that assumption. Legal systems relied on it. Christian theology was built upon it.

In the biblical framework, truth is rooted in the character of God. "Your word is truth," Jesus prays in John 17:17. In John 14:6, He declares, "I am the way, and the truth, and the life." Truth is not described as self-generated or negotiable. It is revealed.

Over the past several decades, however, a measurable shift has taken place in how truth is understood in public life. Increasingly, truth is treated as something internal—validated by personal experience and emotional authenticity. The language of "my truth" and "your truth" has become common in education, therapy, media, and social discourse. While often intended to affirm dignity or lived experience, the phrasing reflects a deeper philosophical transformation: truth is no longer primarily discovered; it is declared.

This shift did not emerge from nowhere. Twentieth-century intellectual movements challenged the idea of universal, objective standards. Postmodern philosophy questioned what French thinker Jean-François Lyotard called "metanarratives"—overarching explanations that claim universal authority. Suspicion toward grand claims about truth filtered gradually into education and media. Over time, skepticism toward objective moral frameworks became culturally mainstream rather than academically confined.

At the same time, expressive individualism—the idea that personal authenticity is discovered inwardly and must be expressed outwardly—gained cultural dominance. Sociologists such as Robert Bellah and historians such as Carl Trueman have documented this transition. Identity increasingly became something self-constructed rather than received from external sources such as family, tradition, religion, or biology. The inward psychological life moved to the center of moral authority.

Technology accelerated the transformation. Social media platforms reward emotional storytelling and identity expression. Algorithms amplify content that generates engagement—often content rooted in personal narrative. Communities form rapidly around shared experiences, reinforcing particular interpretations of identity and morality. In such environments, disagreement is frequently interpreted not merely as error but as invalidation.

The result is not simply disagreement. It is collision.

When truth is objective, two individuals can debate while appealing to a shared standard. They may disagree about interpretation, but they agree that reality exists independently of their preferences. When truth is subjective, disagreement becomes existential. If truth originates in the self, then challenging a claim can feel like challenging a person's identity itself. The emotional stakes rise. Dialogue becomes volatile. Institutions struggle to mediate because there is no agreed-upon authority beyond personal conviction.

This helps explain why debates over gender identity policy escalate so quickly. One side appeals to biological categories and long-standing legal interpretations. The other appeals to lived experience and psychological well-being. Each side believes it is defending justice. Yet beneath the policy language are fundamentally different assumptions about where truth resides.

The same fracture appears in churches. Some congregations reaffirm historic Christian doctrine concerning male and female creation, sexual ethics, and biblical authority. Others seek to emphasize inclusion while reexamining traditional language. Pastors face criticism from opposing directions—accused either of compromise or of intolerance. Beneath these tensions lies the same question: Is truth something revealed by God and binding across time, or something reframed through contemporary understanding?

This is the question beneath the chaos.

The controversies in school districts, corporate boardrooms, legislatures, and churches are not random. They are symptoms of a deeper philosophical transformation. Society no longer shares a common definition of truth. Without that shared foundation, every disagreement becomes harder to resolve.

This book does not aim to inflame the debate. Nor does it attempt to offer political solutions. Its purpose is narrower and more foundational: to examine the shift from objective truth to subjective truth, to evaluate that shift through the lens of Scripture, and to ask whether the language of "my truth" can sustain a coherent society or a faithful church.

Before addressing specific issues—identity, morality, church leadership, family life—we must address the foundation. What is truth? Where does it come from? And who has authority to define it?

Until those questions are answered clearly, the collisions will continue.

How the Shift Developed

The shift described above did not happen suddenly. It developed over decades through identifiable intellectual and cultural changes that gradually reshaped how Western society understands authority, identity, and truth.

In the mid-to-late twentieth century, a number of influential philosophers challenged the assumption that universal truth claims could be trusted. Among them was French thinker Jean-François Lyotard, who described postmodernism as "incredulity toward metanarratives"—a skepticism toward large, overarching explanations that claim authority across cultures and generations. While few people read academic philosophy, its influence filtered steadily into universities, media, and education. Confidence in comprehensive truth claims weakened. Suspicion toward universal moral standards grew.

Importantly, this skepticism did not immediately eliminate belief in truth altogether. Rather, it shifted where authority was located. If no single narrative could claim universal legitimacy, then meaning increasingly became local, contextual, and personal. Truth was not necessarily denied, but it was relativized. What mattered most was not whether a claim corresponded to external reality, but whether it resonated within a particular community or experience.

At the same time, Western culture experienced a parallel transformation in how identity itself was understood. Earlier generations generally regarded identity as shaped by givens—family, nation, religious tradition, biological sex, and inherited moral frameworks. These elements were not always embraced without tension, but they were treated as realities to be navigated rather than raw material to be redesigned.

Over the past several decades, that understanding shifted toward what sociologists call expressive individualism. Under this framework, personal fulfillment is achieved not by conforming to external moral order but by expressing one's inner psychological self. Authenticity—living in alignment with one's internal sense of identity—became a central moral value. The self moved from being formed by external structures to being constructed from internal perception.

This development was not merely theoretical. It reshaped education, entertainment, advertising, and corporate culture. Messages encouraging individuals to "be true to yourself" or "define your own identity" became culturally ubiquitous. Psychological well-being was increasingly framed in terms of self-acceptance and self-expression. In such an environment, external authority—whether religious, biological, or traditional—could appear restrictive rather than formative.

Technological change accelerated these trends dramatically. The widespread adoption of smartphones and social media platforms in the early twenty-first century altered how identity is expressed and reinforced. Online spaces allow individuals to curate narratives about themselves and to find communities that affirm particular understandings of identity. Algorithms prioritize emotionally engaging content, often elevating personal testimony over structured argument. Ideas move rapidly from niche communities into mainstream awareness.

Researchers have documented correlations between increased social media usage and heightened identity-based discourse, particularly among adolescents and young adults. While digital technology did not create expressive individualism, it provided a powerful engine for its amplification. Identity claims can now be shared, affirmed, and defended in real time before a global audience.

As authority moved inward and identity became self-defined, the concept of harm also expanded. In earlier frameworks, harm typically referred to tangible injury—physical violence, legal deprivation, or measurable discrimination. In a culture shaped by expressive individualism, harm increasingly includes psychological invalidation. Disagreement with a person's declared identity can be perceived not merely as error but as denial of dignity.

This development helps explain why contemporary debates escalate quickly. When one party appeals to biological categories, historical precedent, or scriptural authority, and another appeals to lived experience and personal authenticity, they are not merely disagreeing about policy. They are operating from different assumptions about where truth resides. Without shared assumptions about authority, mediation becomes difficult. Each side views the other as fundamentally mistaken about reality itself.

The result is not simply cultural tension but epistemological fragmentation—a breakdown in shared understanding about how truth is determined. Institutions struggle to navigate this fragmentation. Schools attempt to balance parental rights and student autonomy. Courts interpret statutes written under older assumptions about sex and identity. Churches wrestle with how to apply ancient texts within contemporary frameworks that define identity differently.

None of this proves that subjective truth claims are correct or incorrect. It does, however, clarify why the conflict feels so deep. The debate is not merely about individual policies or specific court cases. It concerns the relocation of moral authority—from external revelation and observable reality to internal perception and personal declaration.

When authority moves inward, stability becomes harder to sustain. If truth is primarily self-defined, then disagreement is inherently destabilizing. There is no higher standard to which both parties can appeal. Conflict becomes not a dispute about interpretation but a contest over whose experience defines reality.

The consequences of this relocation are increasingly visible—not only in public institutions but in families, churches, and everyday relationships.

To understand those consequences, we must look more closely at what happens when truth becomes untethered from an external anchor.

When Authority Moves Inward

.   .   .

When truth is untethered from an external anchor, its effects do not remain confined to philosophical debate. They surface in institutional policy, legal conflict, and daily relationships. The consequences are often most visible in moments of public controversy, but they originate in deeper assumptions about authority and identity.

Education has become one of the primary arenas where these assumptions collide. In recent years, multiple states have seen disputes over policies related to gender identity in schools. In Virginia, guidance documents issued during different gubernatorial administrations reflected contrasting approaches to parental notification and student autonomy. In 2021, the Virginia Department of Education released model policies emphasizing protections for transgender students under the Virginia Values Act. In 2022, revised model policies emphasized parental involvement and biological sex distinctions. Local districts responded in varied ways, leading to inconsistent implementation and public tension. Similar conflicts unfolded in New Jersey, where state guidance affirmed gender identity accommodations, and in California and Colorado, where state-level policies expanded gender identity protections.

These policy disputes reveal more than administrative disagreement. They reflect a foundational question: when a student declares an identity, what authority adjudicates that claim? Is it biological sex, parental oversight, psychological well-being, statutory interpretation, or personal self-identification? Each answer presupposes a different understanding of truth.

Healthcare has experienced parallel tension. Over the past decade, medical associations have issued evolving guidelines regarding gender dysphoria and transition-related care for minors. Some organizations have affirmed gender-affirming approaches, while others have urged caution, citing limited long-term data. In the United Kingdom, the 2024 Cass Review—a government-commissioned independent review of gender identity services for children and young people —raised concerns about evidence standards and recommended greater clinical caution. Several European countries subsequently adjusted their protocols regarding puberty blockers and hormone treatments for minors. In the United States, state legislatures have taken divergent paths, with some restricting such treatments for minors and others expanding access.

These developments demonstrate that even within professional and scientific communities, consensus is not uniform. The disagreement is not merely moral; it is epistemological. How should evidence be weighed? What constitutes sufficient proof? Should internal identity experience override biological classification? When institutions answer those questions differently, public trust becomes strained.

The legal system has also been drawn into the debate. Courts have been asked to interpret whether existing civil rights statutes—such as Title IX—apply to gender identity. Federal guidance has shifted across administrations, producing regulatory oscillation. In 2020, the Supreme Court's decision in Bostock v. Clayton County held that Title VII's prohibition of sex discrimination in employment includes discrimination based on sexual orientation and gender identity. While the decision addressed employment law, its reasoning influenced broader policy discussions. Subsequent litigation has addressed how these interpretations apply in educational contexts, athletics, and healthcare.

None of these cases can be reduced to simple political slogans. They reflect competing frameworks about how identity, biology, and law interact. When truth is understood primarily as self-identification, legal language must expand to protect that identification. When truth is understood as rooted in biological categories, statutory interpretation follows a different path.

Religious institutions face similar pressure. Some denominations have reaffirmed historic doctrines regarding male and female creation and sexual ethics. Others have revised statements or allowed local congregations to determine policy. In certain cases, denominational disputes have led to formal schisms. These divisions are not merely about pastoral tone; they concern whether biblical texts describe enduring reality or culturally conditioned perspective.

The Personal Consequences

The consequences are not limited to institutions. Families increasingly report tension over identity questions that would have been rare in previous generations. Surveys show that younger Americans are more likely than older generations to identify as LGBTQ+, reflecting either increased visibility, expanded definitions, greater social acceptance, or some combination of factors. Whatever the cause, generational divergence is measurable. Parents and children often interpret identity language differently because they operate from different philosophical assumptions.

Workplace culture reflects similar dynamics. Many corporations have implemented diversity, equity, and inclusion programs that include gender identity language and pronoun practices. Employees who affirm these practices view them as affirmations of dignity and inclusion. Employees who question them sometimes express concern about compelled speech or conflicts with personal conviction. Human resources departments are left to navigate between anti-discrimination commitments and free expression concerns.

These developments reveal a common thread. The conflict is not primarily about civility or kindness. Most participants across the spectrum affirm the importance of human dignity. The disagreement centers on what defines reality and who has authority to articulate it.

When a society lacks consensus on the source of truth, policy debates become proxies for deeper philosophical disagreement. School board meetings become heated not because citizens suddenly lost the capacity for dialogue, but because they no longer share the same epistemological foundation. One group believes it is defending objective reality. The other believes it is defending personal authenticity and psychological safety. Both may appeal to compassion. Both may claim justice. Yet without agreement on what truth is, resolution becomes elusive.

This fragmentation affects not only public discourse but personal trust. If truth is primarily internal and self-declared, then stability depends on ongoing affirmation. If affirmation falters, identity feels threatened. The emotional intensity surrounding contemporary debates reflects this vulnerability. When identity rests on subjective declaration, disagreement carries existential weight.

None of this analysis dismisses the complexity of human experience. Psychological distress is real. Social ostracism is real. Historical injustices are real. The question is not whether individuals deserve dignity. The question is whether dignity requires redefining truth itself.

The movement from objective truth to subjective truth promises empowerment. It offers individuals authority over their own narrative. Yet it also produces instability. If truth changes with perception, then certainty becomes fragile. Institutions must continually adapt to shifting self-definitions. Legal language expands to accommodate new categories. Public discourse grows more volatile.

The consequences of relocating truth from external authority to internal perception are not confined to legislatures, school boards, or courtrooms. They surface in ordinary conversations and everyday relationships.

When truth is self-defined, disagreement becomes personal. If a moral claim is grounded in biology, Scripture, or historical precedent, it can be evaluated against those standards. But if a moral claim is grounded in personal identity, then contradiction feels like rejection of the self. The shift changes the emotional temperature of discourse. What was once debate becomes perceived invalidation.

This dynamic affects friendships, workplaces, and families. Parents and children may use the same words—identity, authenticity, dignity —while meaning fundamentally different things. Coworkers may interpret policy disagreements not as intellectual difference but as moral hostility. Online discussions escalate quickly because participants are not merely defending ideas; they are defending identities.

The erosion of objective truth also reshapes moral reasoning. If truth originates internally, then moral boundaries become fluid. What feels authentic becomes authoritative. External constraints—religious doctrine, biological categories, inherited tradition—are judged by whether they align with self-perception. Stability becomes difficult because the standard itself shifts.

This does not eliminate moral conviction. In fact, it often intensifies it. Individuals who ground truth in internal identity can hold their convictions with deep sincerity. The issue is not passion; it is foundation. When two individuals hold incompatible truths rooted in personal authority, there is no shared reference point for resolution. Conflict is settled not by appeal to reality but by negotiation of influence, social pressure, or institutional power.

In such an environment, tolerance becomes fragile. If disagreement is equated with harm, then pluralism becomes unsustainable. Institutions must choose which truth claims to affirm. Legal systems must decide which identities receive protection. Educational systems must determine which frameworks shape curriculum. The question shifts from "What is true?" to "Whose truth prevails?"

This shift has significant implications for freedom. Historically, free societies have depended on the assumption that truth exists independently of the individual and can be pursued through reasoned dialogue. If truth is primarily self-declared, then speech that contradicts self-declaration may be perceived as inherently harmful. The boundary between disagreement and discrimination becomes contested. The language of rights expands, but shared understanding contracts.

The consequences extend beyond social order to personal stability. If identity rests solely on internal perception, it must be continually reinforced. External affirmation becomes essential. When affirmation falters, uncertainty follows. The burden of self-definition can become heavy. A framework that promises empowerment may also produce fragility, because it lacks an anchor beyond the self.

None of this analysis suggests that human experience is insignificant. Personal narratives matter. Psychological distress is real. Compassion is essential. The question is not whether individuals deserve dignity. The question is whether dignity requires redefining truth as subjective.

If truth is fluid, then it cannot anchor. If truth changes with perception, then it cannot stabilize community. If truth is self-generated, then no claim can ultimately bind beyond personal preference.

This leads to the central question of our time: Is truth something we create, or something we receive?

The biblical worldview answers that question unambiguously. Truth is not invented. It is revealed. It is not constructed from internal feeling. It flows from the character of God. It is not validated by consensus. It stands whether affirmed or denied.

This claim is not new. It predates modern philosophy and contemporary politics. It is rooted in the conviction that reality itself is grounded in a Creator who defines what is good, true, and just. In that framework, truth does not threaten dignity; it secures it. Identity is not self-constructed; it is bestowed. Authority is not inwardly generated; it is divinely given.

If that foundation is true, then the instability we are witnessing is not surprising. A structure cannot remain stable once its base is removed. The cultural conflicts over gender, morality, authority, and speech are not isolated controversies. They are symptoms of a deeper displacement.

The task, then, is not merely to win arguments or refine policy. It is to recover a coherent understanding of truth itself.

Before we address specific moral questions, before we examine identity, family, church, or public life, we must ask what Scripture means when it speaks of truth. We must examine whether truth is absolute and revealed, or whether it is malleable and self-defined.

The Foundational Question

The rest of this book proceeds from that foundation.

If truth is objective and grounded in God, then it has authority over every human claim. If truth is subjective and internally generated, then authority rests within the individual. There is no neutral middle ground.

The collision we see in our institutions is the outward expression of that deeper divide.

To move forward, we must return to first principles.

What is truth?

And who has the authority to define it?

Chapter 2 begins there.

2

TRUTH IS NOT SELF-DEFINED

If the central fracture of our time concerns the nature of truth, then clarity requires returning to first principles. Before evaluating policy, culture, or personal identity, we must ask what Scripture means when it speaks of truth. The biblical worldview does not treat truth as abstract theory or private sentiment. It presents truth as grounded in the character of God, revealed in His Word, and embodied in Jesus Christ.

In contemporary discourse, truth is often described as something constructed. Individuals "find their truth" or "speak their truth." In contrast, the Bible consistently portrays truth as something given. It originates outside the human will. It does not emerge from emotional authenticity. It is disclosed by a Creator who defines reality.

The Old Testament frames truth within the character of God Himself. Numbers 23:19 declares, "God is not man, that he should lie." The statement is not merely about divine honesty; it reflects a deeper claim about divine reliability. God's nature is not shifting. His words are not strategic manipulations. Truth is inseparable from who He is. Psalm 119 repeatedly affirms this connection: "The sum of your word is truth, and every one of your righteous rules endures forever" (Psalm 119:160). Truth is enduring because its source is enduring.

This understanding stands in contrast to cultural frameworks that treat truth as provisional or evolving. In Scripture, truth does not adjust itself to accommodate preference. It is not negotiated by majority vote. It is not validated by emotional resonance. It remains stable because it reflects the unchanging nature of God.

Truth Embodied in Christ

The New Testament sharpens this claim. In John 17:17, Jesus prays, "Sanctify them in the truth; your word is truth." The statement is direct and unqualified. God's Word is not merely inspiring or helpful. It is truth itself. In John 14:6, Jesus makes an even more exclusive claim: "I am the way, and the truth, and the life." The claim is not pluralistic. He does not describe Himself as a truth among many. He identifies Himself as the truth.

These passages are foundational because they locate truth in revelation rather than perception. If truth is revealed, then it precedes human interpretation. Individuals may misunderstand it. Cultures may resist it. But they do not create it.

This distinction carries significant implications. If truth is external and revealed, then human flourishing depends on alignment with it. In the biblical framework, freedom is not self-definition; it is conformity to reality as God has made it. Jesus connects truth and freedom explicitly: "You will know the truth, and the truth will set you free" (John 8:32). Freedom is the result of knowing what is real, not the power to redefine what is real.

Modern culture often reverses this relationship. Freedom is framed as autonomy—the capacity to define oneself without external constraint. Under that definition, truth can appear restrictive. Yet Scripture presents constraint differently. Moral boundaries are not arbitrary limitations; they are guardrails aligned with reality. A command does not create truth; it reflects it.

Truth and Creation Order

The biblical narrative begins with creation. Genesis 1 describes a world ordered by divine speech. God speaks, and reality takes form. Light and darkness are distinguished. Land and sea are separated. Male and female are created as embodied categories within that order. The text presents structure, distinction, and intentional design. Truth, in this context, is not an afterthought. It is woven into creation itself.

This order is not merely physical; it is moral. Genesis 2–3 introduces the first recorded challenge to divine authority. The serpent's question—"Did God actually say?"—is not simply about a rule. It is about the reliability of revelation. The temptation offered to Eve includes the promise of autonomy: "You will be like God, knowing good and evil" (Genesis 3:5). The appeal is not ignorance but self-determination. The implication is that humans can define moral reality independently.

The pattern is instructive. The first rupture in the biblical account is not primarily behavioral; it is epistemological. Authority shifts from God's word to human judgment. The result is fragmentation—between humanity and God, between man and woman, and within the self. The narrative suggests that when truth is detached from divine revelation, disorder follows.

Throughout Scripture, this theme recurs. Proverbs 14:12 warns, "There is a way that seems right to a man, but its end is the way to death." The warning is not anti-reason; it is anti-autonomy. Human perception alone is insufficient as the final authority. Jeremiah 17:9 describes the heart as "deceitful above all things." The point is not cynicism about emotion but caution about elevating it to ultimate authority.

None of these passages deny the complexity of human experience. They acknowledge that perception can be sincere. The question is whether sincerity determines truth. Scripture consistently answers no.

This biblical framework stands in direct tension with expressive individualism. If identity is primarily self-constructed and truth is internally validated, then external revelation becomes optional. Scripture, however, presents revelation as normative. It does not invite individuals to negotiate its claims according to preference. It calls for trust and obedience.

The contrast between these frameworks is not minor. It shapes how one understands identity, morality, authority, and community. If truth is revealed and stable, then disagreement can be evaluated against that standard. If truth is internally generated, then disagreement becomes a threat to self-definition.

The stakes are therefore high. The debate over truth is not academic. It determines whether Scripture functions as authority or inspiration. It determines whether moral claims bind universally or vary individually. It determines whether freedom means autonomy or alignment with created reality.

Before applying biblical teaching to specific contemporary issues, the foundation must be clear. The Christian claim is not that believers possess private truth. It is that God has revealed truth that stands over every human perspective. That revelation is not dependent on cultural affirmation. It does not gain legitimacy through popularity. It remains what it is because God remains who He is.

If that claim is false, then the cultural shift toward subjective truth may be a natural progression. If that claim is true, then the shift represents not liberation but detachment from reality itself.

The remainder of this chapter will examine more closely how Scripture describes truth, how it relates to human identity, and why its stability matters in an age of fragmentation.

If Scripture grounds truth in the character of God, then truth is not merely a proposition; it is relational. It flows from who God is. The Bible repeatedly connects truth to divine faithfulness. Deuteronomy 32:4 describes God as "a God of faithfulness and without iniquity, just and upright is he." Psalm 31:5 calls Him "the God of truth." These descriptions are not abstract theological claims. They establish that truth is stable because its source is stable.

This stability distinguishes biblical truth from cultural relativism. Cultural norms shift. Public opinion evolves. Majorities change. But Scripture presents God as unchanging: "For I the Lord do not change" (Malachi 3:6). The immutability of God underwrites the immutability of truth. If God's character does not fluctuate, then the moral reality grounded in His character does not fluctuate.

The New Testament intensifies this claim through the person of Christ. John's Gospel opens with a theological declaration: "In the beginning was the Word, and the Word was with God, and the Word was God" (John 1:1). Later, John writes, "The Word became flesh and dwelt among us, and we have seen his glory... full of grace and truth" (John 1:14). Truth is not merely spoken by Christ; it is embodied in Him. The life, teaching, death, and resurrection of Jesus are presented as the definitive revelation of reality as God sees it.

This embodiment matters because it prevents truth from becoming merely doctrinal abstraction. Truth in Scripture is not cold assertion. It is inseparable from grace. John intentionally pairs the two: "grace and truth." They are not competitors. They are companions.

This pairing addresses one of the most common modern objections: that claims of absolute truth are inherently intolerant. In contemporary discourse, exclusivity is often equated with hostility. If one claim is true, others must be false. That reality can feel threatening in pluralistic societies. However, Scripture does not present truth as a tool for domination but as a means of liberation.

Jesus connects truth to freedom in John 8:31–32: "If you abide in my word, you are truly my disciples, and you will know the truth, and the truth will set you free." Freedom, in this context, is not autonomy from moral structure. It is deliverance from deception and sin. The bondage described in the passage is not political but spiritual. Truth exposes illusion. It aligns human perception with divine reality.

The biblical vision of truth therefore differs fundamentally from coercion. Coercion forces compliance through power. Truth invites alignment through revelation. The apostle Paul writes in 2 Corinthians 4:2 that believers "refuse to practice cunning or to tamper with God's word, but by the open statement of the truth we would commend ourselves to everyone's conscience in the sight of God." The method is not manipulation but proclamation.

It is important to recognize that Scripture anticipates resistance to truth. In Romans 1:18, Paul speaks of those who "suppress the truth in unrighteousness." The implication is not that truth is unclear, but that it can be resisted. This resistance does not invalidate truth; it confirms human capacity to reject what is revealed.

At the same time, Scripture warns believers against wielding truth without love. Ephesians 4:15 instructs Christians to speak "the truth in love." The command assumes both are necessary. Truth without love becomes harsh. Love without truth becomes sentimentality. The biblical model does not permit separation.

The relationship between truth and love is central in an age that often treats them as opposites. Many assume that affirming another person's self-understanding is the highest form of love. Scripture, however, defines love differently. In 1 Corinthians 13:6, Paul writes that love "does not rejoice at wrongdoing, but rejoices with the truth." Love is not indifferent to reality. It celebrates alignment with it.

This distinction matters because it reframes what compassion means. Compassion does not require agreement with every self-claim. It requires genuine concern for human flourishing. If truth corresponds to how God designed reality, then truth is not the enemy of well-being but its foundation.

Another common objection asserts that claims of absolute truth suppress diversity. Yet diversity and truth are not mutually exclusive. The early Christian church included Jews and Gentiles, slaves and free, men and women (Galatians 3:28). Unity was not built on uniform background but on shared submission to revealed truth. Diversity flourished within a common theological framework.

The alternative—complete relativism—does not eliminate hierarchy; it relocates it. If there is no objective standard, then power determines which truth claims dominate public life. Without an external anchor, institutions default to prevailing cultural currents. The absence of absolute truth does not create neutrality; it creates instability.

The biblical account insists that truth is not oppressive but protective. Psalm 19:7 describes the law of the Lord as "perfect, reviving the soul." Verse 8 calls the precepts of the Lord "right, rejoicing the heart." The commands of God are not portrayed as arbitrary restrictions but as life-giving guidance aligned with created reality.

This perspective challenges modern assumptions. If truth is defined by internal authenticity, then external commands appear restrictive. If truth is defined by divine revelation, then commands function as instruction manuals for flourishing.

The distinction ultimately comes down to authority. Who has the right to define reality? Scripture answers that question unequivocally: the Creator does. Genesis presents God as the One who speaks the world into existence. Job 38–41 depicts God questioning Job about the foundations of the earth, underscoring the Creator-creature distinction. Isaiah 45:9 warns, "Woe to him who strives with him who formed him." The biblical narrative consistently resists the idea that human beings occupy the position of ultimate authority.

This does not diminish human dignity. On the contrary, Scripture grounds dignity in creation: "So God created man in his own image" (Genesis 1:27). Identity is bestowed, not constructed. Worth is inherent, not negotiated. The doctrine of the image of God provides a stable basis for human value without requiring self-definition.

If truth is rooted in the character of God, revealed in Scripture, and embodied in Christ, then it is neither arbitrary nor oppressive. It is consistent, coherent, and trustworthy. The instability seen in contemporary debates is not evidence that truth is harmful. It is evidence that truth has been detached from its source.

The question, then, is not whether absolute truth exists. It is whether the God who reveals Himself in Scripture is who He claims to be. If He is, then truth is not self-defined. It is received.

The next step is to examine how this revealed truth speaks specifically to identity and moral order—areas where the cultural shift has been most pronounced.

If truth is revealed and grounded in the character of God, then it necessarily speaks to the structure of human identity. Scripture does not present identity as self-originating. It presents identity as created, embodied, and relational.

The opening chapters of Genesis establish this framework. Genesis 1 describes a world formed through divine speech. Order precedes humanity. Distinction precedes identity. Light and darkness are separated. Land and sea are distinguished. Vegetation, animals, and finally humanity are brought into being according to God's design. Creation is not chaotic; it is structured.

Within that structure, humanity is described as uniquely bearing God's image: "So God created man in his own image, in the image of God he created him; male and female he created them" (Genesis 1:27). The verse is brief but foundational. Human identity is presented as both dignified and differentiated. The text does not treat maleness and femaleness as interchangeable constructs but as embodied realities within creation order.

Genesis 2 reinforces this embodiment. The man is formed from the dust of the ground; the woman is formed from the man's side. The narrative emphasizes physicality. Humanity is not presented as a detached consciousness inhabiting a disposable body. Body and identity are intertwined. The declaration that creation is "very good" (Genesis 1:31) applies to this embodied differentiation.

Identity as Received, Not Constructed

The biblical account therefore roots identity in something prior to individual perception. Identity is received before it is interpreted. It is given before it is expressed.

This does not deny complexity within human experience. Scripture acknowledges suffering, confusion, and distortion resulting from the Fall in Genesis 3. The rupture introduced by sin affects every dimension of life, including relationships, desires, and self-understanding. The Bible does not portray humanity as psychologically simplistic. It portrays humanity as fallen.

However, the Fall does not erase creation. It distorts it. Redemption in Scripture does not involve the reinvention of human nature but its restoration. Paul writes in Colossians 1:16 that "by him all things were created." Later, in Colossians 1:18, he describes Christ as the beginning, the firstborn from the dead—implying renewal, not replacement, of creation's design.

When modern culture frames identity as primarily self-determined, it implicitly detaches identity from creation order. The internal sense of self becomes authoritative over the embodied reality of the person. In contrast, Scripture maintains continuity between the body and identity. The body is not an obstacle to authenticity; it is part of God's design.

This connection shapes moral teaching as well. The New Testament addresses sexual ethics not as arbitrary rule-making but as alignment with created reality. In 1 Corinthians 6:13, Paul writes, "The body is not meant for sexual immorality, but for the Lord, and the Lord for the body." The argument is theological before it is behavioral. The body has purpose because it has a Creator.

Later in the same chapter, Paul asks rhetorically, "Do you not know that your body is a temple of the Holy Spirit within you?" (1 Corinthians 6:19). The appeal is not to preference but to identity grounded in divine ownership. Christian moral reasoning flows from theological anthropology—from what human beings are, not merely what they feel.

The same pattern appears in Romans 1. Paul describes a cultural exchange: "They exchanged the truth about God for a lie" (Romans 1:25). The consequence of this exchange is described not only in spiritual terms but in relational and moral terms. The passage has generated extensive debate, but its central claim is clear: when truth about God is displaced, human behavior follows.

This is not presented as mere rule violation. It is presented as misalignment with reality. The language of "exchange" is important. Something true is substituted for something false. The issue is not authenticity but accuracy.

Critics sometimes argue that appeals to creation order are simplistic or insensitive to lived experience. Scripture does not minimize the complexity of human struggle. The Psalms are filled with lament. The prophets speak of anguish and exile. The New Testament recognizes weakness and temptation. Yet complexity does not nullify structure. Emotional intensity does not redefine ontology.

This distinction is crucial. A person may experience profound internal conflict. That experience deserves compassion and careful listening. But compassion does not require redefining what Scripture describes as created reality. The biblical approach holds two truths simultaneously: human beings are deeply valued, and human perception is not ultimate authority.

The resurrection further reinforces the dignity of embodiment. Christian hope is not escape from physical existence but the redemption of it. In 1 Corinthians 15, Paul argues for the future resurrection of the body. The Christian vision does not treat the body as disposable. It anticipates its renewal. This theological commitment challenges any framework that treats embodiment as incidental to identity.

The doctrine of creation also establishes limits. If God is Creator and humanity is creature, then autonomy is not absolute. Isaiah 45:9 warns against the clay disputing with the potter. The imagery underscores dependence. Freedom in Scripture is not independence from design but alignment with it.

This vision stands in contrast to modern assumptions that equate authenticity with self-definition. Under expressive individualism, the highest moral good is coherence between internal feeling and external expression. Under the biblical framework, the highest good is faithfulness to divine design.

These frameworks inevitably produce different conclusions about identity and morality. The disagreement is not primarily about kindness or dignity. It is about authority.

If identity is self-constructed, then internal conviction defines truth. If identity is created, then truth precedes conviction. The first framework prioritizes autonomy. The second prioritizes revelation.

The implications extend beyond sexuality or gender. They affect how one understands vocation, marriage, family, and community. Scripture presents marriage as a covenantal union between male and female (Genesis 2:24; Matthew 19:4–6). It presents family as a context for formation rather than self-invention. It describes the church as a body with differentiated roles (1 Corinthians 12). In each case, identity is relational and structured.

When these structures are reinterpreted through subjective truth, stability weakens. If roles are negotiable according to personal preference rather than revealed design, communal coherence becomes difficult. The biblical model does not eliminate individuality, but it situates individuality within created order.

This is not an argument for rigidity or lack of empathy. It is an argument for coherence. A worldview that detaches identity from creation must continually renegotiate its categories. A worldview that roots identity in revelation possesses a stable reference point.

The modern emphasis on self-definition often emerges from legitimate concerns—desire for dignity, recognition, and relief from suffering. Scripture affirms those desires but locates their fulfillment differently. Human worth is grounded in being made in the image of God. Meaning is grounded in relationship to the Creator. Restoration is grounded in redemption through Christ.

The question, therefore, is not whether identity matters. It is whether identity is self-defined or God-given.

If Scripture is correct, then truth about identity does not originate within us. It is received from the One who made us.

In the next section, we will consider how this revealed truth interacts with compassion, pastoral care, and the realities of a pluralistic society.

Truth in a Pluralistic World

If truth is revealed and rooted in the character of God, a practical question immediately follows: How does such a claim function in a pluralistic society? Modern Western culture contains multiple religious and philosophical frameworks. To assert that truth is absolute and divinely revealed can sound exclusionary in a setting that prizes diversity.

Scripture does not deny pluralism as a social reality. The early church existed within the Roman Empire—a setting marked by religious diversity, competing philosophies, and state power. Christians did not respond by attempting to eliminate disagreement. They responded by proclaiming what they believed to be true while living peaceably where possible. Paul writes in Romans 12:18, "If possible, so far as it depends on you, live peaceably with all." The command assumes coexistence amid disagreement.

At the same time, the early church did not dilute its truth claims to avoid offense. In Acts 4:12, Peter declares of Christ, "There is salvation in no one else." That claim is exclusive, yet it is presented not as hostility but as conviction. The Christian approach to pluralism, therefore, is not coercion but witness. It does not demand that all affirm biblical truth. It maintains that truth remains true regardless of affirmation.

This distinction matters. Affirming absolute truth does not require controlling others. It requires faithfulness to what one believes God has revealed. The New Testament consistently frames the church's role in these terms. First Timothy 3:15 describes the church as "a pillar and buttress of the truth." The imagery is architectural. A pillar supports. A buttress stabilizes. The church is not described as inventing truth but upholding it.

This responsibility carries weight in an age where institutions are uncertain about foundational claims. If cultural consensus on truth is weakening, the church cannot rely on societal reinforcement. It must be anchored in Scripture. Second Timothy 3:16–17 declares, "All Scripture is breathed out by God and profitable for teaching, for reproof, for correction, and for training in righteousness." The authority of Scripture is not contingent on cultural approval. It derives from divine origin.

Holding to revealed truth does not eliminate compassion. On the contrary, it clarifies it. If truth corresponds to created reality, then misalignment with truth carries consequences. Love, in the biblical sense, involves guiding others toward what is real. James 5:19–20 speaks of turning someone back from error as an act of rescue. The assumption is that error is not neutral. It has trajectory.

At the same time, Scripture warns against pride in defending truth. First Corinthians 8:1 cautions, "Knowledge puffs up, but love builds up." The possession of correct doctrine does not justify arrogance.

Truth must be accompanied by humility, because understanding itself is a gift. Christians are not self-generated guardians of insight; they are recipients of revelation.

This humility is essential in contemporary engagement. In public debate, it is possible to defend biblical truth in ways that mirror the hostility of the surrounding culture. The New Testament calls for a different posture. First Peter 3:15 instructs believers to be prepared to give a reason for their hope "yet do it with gentleness and respect." Conviction and gentleness are not contradictory. They are complementary.

The stability offered by revealed truth does not remove complexity from human experience. Christians live in communities with neighbors, colleagues, and family members who do not share their convictions. The biblical model does not demand withdrawal from society. It calls for faithful presence within it. Jeremiah 29:7, though addressed to exiles in Babylon, captures the principle: "Seek the welfare of the city where I have sent you." Engagement and distinction coexist.

What revealed truth does provide is coherence. It offers a framework in which identity, morality, and community are not continually renegotiated. It grounds dignity in the image of God. It grounds morality in creation order. It grounds hope in redemption through Christ. These anchors do not eliminate suffering or disagreement, but they prevent fragmentation from becoming ultimate.

The cultural movement toward subjective truth promises empowerment but often produces uncertainty. If identity must be continually asserted and defended, it remains vulnerable. If moral standards are internally defined, they shift with perception. Scripture offers an alternative vision: identity received rather than constructed, truth revealed rather than negotiated, freedom found in alignment rather than autonomy.

The tension between these visions will not disappear. It is rooted in competing understandings of authority. The question is not whether society will operate with truth claims. It inevitably will. The question is which foundation will sustain them.

If God is the source of truth, then human flourishing depends on conformity to His design. If truth is self-defined, then coherence depends on collective affirmation. One framework rests on revelation. The other rests on consensus.

The Christian claim is clear: truth is not self-defined. It is given.

The next chapter will examine how the shift toward subjective truth reshapes identity, morality, and community at a practical level—and why recovering a coherent understanding of truth is essential for both personal stability and cultural clarity.

3

WHEN TRUTH BECOMES PERSONAL

The debate over truth does not remain abstract for long. What begins as philosophical disagreement eventually shapes how individuals understand themselves, relate to others, and make moral decisions. The shift from objective truth to subjective truth moves quickly from lecture halls to living rooms. It becomes personal.

Over the past several decades, the language of self-definition has become normalized in public discourse. Phrases such as "live your truth," "be true to yourself," and "own your narrative" are framed as moral imperatives. They suggest that authenticity—defined as alignment with one's internal perception—is the highest good. To question that internal perception is often interpreted not as disagreement but as harm.

This shift did not arise from nowhere. It reflects a broader cultural movement often described as expressive individualism. Within this framework, identity is not primarily something discovered within an existing order; it is something constructed from within. The self becomes the central authority.

Earlier generations tended to view identity as largely received. One was born into a family, a biological sex, a cultural tradition, and often a religious framework. These givens were not always experienced as comforting, and they were certainly not immune from abuse or distortion. Yet they provided a structure within which meaning was interpreted. Personal freedom existed, but it operated within boundaries that were assumed to correspond to reality.

Today, those boundaries are frequently treated as optional. Biological categories are described as fluid. Moral expectations are considered socially constructed. Even long-standing religious doctrines are evaluated primarily through the lens of personal resonance. Authority is no longer measured by historical continuity or transcendent grounding but by internal affirmation.

The consequences of this relocation of authority are significant. When identity is primarily self-defined, stability depends on the maintenance of that definition. Identity must be asserted, defended, and validated. External disagreement is no longer simply intellectual; it can feel existential. To question a claim about the self is perceived as questioning the person.

This dynamic reshapes relationships. Conversations that once revolved around shared standards now revolve around personal narratives. Disagreement is no longer mediated by appeal to common authority but negotiated through emotional impact. Words take on heightened significance because they are tied directly to self-conception.

The psychological weight of this shift is often underestimated. Self-definition promises empowerment. It appears to grant autonomy and agency. Yet it also places enormous responsibility on the individual. If the self is the ultimate source of identity, then coherence depends on continual internal certainty. Doubt becomes destabilizing. External critique becomes threatening.

Social media has accelerated this process. Platforms reward visibility and personal storytelling. Identity becomes performative as well as internal. Affirmation is quantified through engagement metrics. The self is not only constructed but broadcast.

This does not mean that every expression of personal identity is misguided or insincere. Many individuals articulate their experiences with genuine conviction. The issue is not sincerity. The issue is foundation. If identity is grounded solely in perception, it remains vulnerable to change and conflict. If identity is received within a created order, it rests on something more stable than emotion or affirmation.

The biblical account begins not with self-construction but with creation. In Genesis 1:27, humanity is described as made in the image of God—male and female. Identity is presented as gift rather than invention. It is received before it is expressed. Dignity flows from divine intention, not internal declaration.

This framework does not erase individuality. Scripture affirms personality, calling, and uniqueness. Yet it situates those expressions within a prior reality. The self is not ultimate; God is.

The contrast between these frameworks—self-defined identity versus received identity—lies at the center of contemporary tension. When culture encourages individuals to look inward for ultimate authority while Scripture directs them outward and upward, conflict is inevitable.

The shift toward internal authority may feel liberating at first, but its long-term implications are profound. If every individual defines identity independently, shared moral language weakens. Community cohesion depends increasingly on mutual affirmation rather than shared conviction.

Truth, in this environment, becomes relational rather than referential. It is validated by agreement rather than correspondence to reality. What matters most is not whether a claim aligns with created order but whether it affirms the individual making it.

The question, then, is not merely philosophical. It is deeply personal: What happens to a society when identity becomes untethered from an external anchor?

.   .   .

Identity as Self-Expression

Expressive individualism rests on a simple but powerful premise: the authentic self is discovered internally and must be expressed externally. To suppress that expression is to live dishonestly. Within this framework, society's role is not to shape identity but to affirm it. Institutions exist to protect self-definition rather than to guide it.

This assumption reshapes moral reasoning. If the highest good is authenticity, then any boundary that limits self-expression appears inherently suspect. Traditions, religious doctrines, and even biological realities may be interpreted as constraints imposed by others rather than truths to be received. The internal voice becomes the final arbiter.

The appeal of this framework is understandable. It promises liberation from oppressive systems. It affirms the value of personal experience. It validates emotional reality. In cultures where institutional trust has declined, inward authority can feel safer than external control.

Yet the movement from receiving identity to constructing identity introduces instability. Construction requires maintenance. What is built can be revised. If identity rests on internal perception alone, then changes in perception can unsettle the entire structure. The self becomes a project rather than a given.

This instability affects moral language. When identity is fluid, moral categories often follow. Actions are evaluated primarily by their impact on personal fulfillment rather than their alignment with enduring standards. "Does this reflect who I am?" replaces "Is this right?" as the governing question.

The tension becomes especially visible in areas of sexuality and embodiment. For centuries, biological sex was understood as an objective feature of human existence. Contemporary discourse increasingly distinguishes between biological sex and gender identity, framing the latter as rooted in psychological experience rather than physical reality. Whatever one's position in these debates, the underlying philosophical shift is clear: internal perception carries decisive authority.

This pattern extends beyond gender. Career choices, relational commitments, and belief systems are all increasingly evaluated through the lens of personal authenticity. Even faith can be reframed as an extension of self-expression rather than submission to divine revelation. Religious affiliation becomes meaningful only insofar as it resonates internally.

The biblical narrative offers a different orientation. Identity begins not with inward assertion but with divine declaration. Before Adam and Eve speak, they are named. Before they act, they are described as image-bearers. Their worth is established externally by God's creative act. They do not define themselves into existence.

This distinction does not eliminate agency. Scripture calls individuals to obedience, repentance, and faith—actions that require personal choice. But those choices occur within a reality already established by God. Freedom operates within creation, not against it.

When identity is severed from creation order, moral reasoning loses its anchor. If the self defines its own boundaries, there is no higher appeal when those boundaries conflict. Resolution depends on negotiation or power rather than shared truth.

The result is a culture marked by heightened sensitivity. Words become charged because they are interpreted through identity. Disagreement is often recast as harm. The social expectation shifts from tolerance of difference to affirmation of self-definition. Refusal to affirm is perceived as rejection.

Communities struggle under this pressure. Schools, workplaces, and churches must determine how to navigate competing identity claims. Attempts to maintain historical definitions are labeled exclusionary. Attempts to redefine categories create tension for those who view such changes as departures from reality.

The deeper issue is not political alignment but epistemology—how we know what is true. If knowledge is grounded primarily in subjective experience, then disagreement becomes nearly impossible to adjudicate. Each person's perception carries equal authority.

This raises a crucial question: Can a society sustain coherence when identity is entirely self-constructed? Or does stability require a shared understanding of reality that precedes personal declaration?

The cultural experiment continues to unfold. Its outcomes are visible not only in legislation and media but in everyday relationships. Parents and children navigate generational divides. Friends negotiate language and expectations. Churches wrestle with doctrine and compassion.

The tension is not likely to diminish. As long as internal perception is treated as ultimate authority, the collision between self-defined identity and revealed truth will remain.

Morality Without an Anchor

When truth becomes personal, morality inevitably follows. If there is no external authority grounding right and wrong, ethical standards shift toward either individual preference or collective consensus. Both appear workable in theory. Both prove fragile in practice.

Moral claims persist in modern culture. Language about justice, equality, and dignity remains strong. Yet the grounding of those claims is increasingly detached from transcendent reference points. Appeals to divine authority are often replaced with appeals to autonomy or social agreement.

Historically, much of Western moral reasoning was shaped by the conviction that human beings are created in the image of God. This belief provided a stable basis for human dignity. Worth did not depend on achievement, affirmation, or majority approval. It was inherent.

When that theological foundation is removed, dignity must be justified elsewhere. Some appeal to evolutionary development, others to social contracts, and still others to individual autonomy. Each offers partial insight, but none carries the same transcendent authority as divine creation.

Without an external anchor, moral disputes are settled through negotiation of influence. If two parties disagree, there is no higher standard to which both must submit. Resolution depends on persuasion, legal force, or social pressure.

This does not produce immediate collapse. Societies can function for extended periods on inherited moral capital. Norms persist even after their foundations erode. But over time, questions emerge: Why is one moral vision binding and another optional? On what basis can one self-defined standard be judged harmful while another is celebrated?

When morality becomes self-generated, obligation weakens. Duty feels imposed rather than discovered. Sacrifice becomes negotiable. Commitment depends on continued personal satisfaction.

The biblical vision again offers contrast. Moral law flows from the character of God. It is not arbitrary decree but expression of divine goodness. To violate moral order is not merely to break a rule but to depart from reality as designed.

This understanding reframes obedience. It is not submission to external oppression but alignment with created purpose. Boundaries are not restrictions for their own sake but protections that preserve flourishing.

The cultural shift toward subjective morality promises compassion and flexibility. In some cases, it has exposed genuine injustice. Yet flexibility without foundation can become confusion. When moral categories are endlessly revised, trust erodes.

The question is not whether compassion matters. It does. The question is whether compassion can endure without truth. If moral standards are entirely internal, they shift with emotion. If they are grounded in reality beyond the self, they provide stability even when feelings fluctuate.

The erosion of shared moral authority intensifies cultural conflict. Competing frameworks cannot be reconciled without appeal to something higher than individual preference. Without that appeal, society oscillates between tolerance and coercion.

The consequences are increasingly visible. Moral language grows louder even as moral agreement shrinks. The tension is not accidental. It flows from the relocation of truth.

Authority and the Erosion of Trust

As truth shifts inward, authority inevitably weakens outward. Institutions that once commanded broad cultural trust now operate under suspicion. Churches, universities, courts, media organizations, and even medical associations are frequently viewed not as guardians of wisdom but as competitors for narrative control.

Some of this skepticism is understandable. Institutions are composed of fallible people. History records failures and abuses. Yet when authority itself is treated as inherently illegitimate, society enters unstable territory. If no external voice carries weight beyond personal perception, coherence becomes difficult to sustain.

The modern instinct is to authenticate claims through experience rather than tradition. "My story" becomes more persuasive than historical consensus. Personal narrative carries moral authority in ways that institutional expertise does not. Lived experience becomes the final court of appeal.

This shift changes how truth is evaluated. Expertise is questioned not on the basis of evidence alone but on perceived alignment with identity claims. A statement may be dismissed not because it lacks support but because it challenges internal perception. In such an environment, disagreement is easily interpreted as hostility.

Technology accelerates this pattern. Social media platforms amplify emotionally compelling narratives and reward engagement over coherence. Algorithms prioritize what provokes reaction. Nuance struggles to compete with certainty. Communities form around shared perception rather than shared investigation.

The result is fragmentation. Individuals curate information streams that reinforce preexisting beliefs. Authority is decentralized and personalized. Influencers replace institutions. Online consensus can form rapidly and dissolve just as quickly.

Trust erodes not only between institutions and individuals but between neighbors. When no shared authority exists, disputes cannot be resolved through appeal to common standards. Every disagreement becomes a negotiation of competing realities.

The church is not immune to this dynamic. Congregations must navigate cultural pressures while remaining anchored in revealed truth. Leaders are asked to balance compassion with conviction. Members wrestle with how to speak truthfully without being perceived as harmful.

In such a context, clarity becomes costly. To affirm that truth is objective is to resist a cultural current. Yet to abandon that affirmation is to surrender coherence. The church must decide whether it will mirror the culture's inward turn or stand upon external revelation.

This decision has consequences. When churches redefine doctrine to align with prevailing sentiment, they may experience temporary relief from cultural tension. But relief is not the same as faithfulness. If truth is revealed rather than constructed, then altering doctrine to match perception risks detaching belief from reality.

Authority grounded in revelation does not eliminate humility. Scripture repeatedly calls believers to gentleness, patience, and love. But humility does not require surrender of conviction. It requires recognizing that conviction rests not on personal preference but on divine disclosure.

The erosion of authority in broader culture intensifies the church's responsibility. First Timothy 3:15 describes the church as "a pillar and buttress of the truth." A pillar supports. A buttress stabilizes. The imagery implies that truth exists independently of the structure that upholds it. The church does not create truth; it preserves and proclaims it.

When truth becomes internalized at the cultural level, the church's role becomes more countercultural. It must articulate a vision of authority rooted not in power but in revelation. This posture will not satisfy every critic. It was never intended to.

The Psychological Cost of Self-Created Truth

The inward relocation of authority is often presented as therapeutic. It promises freedom from external judgment. It assures individuals that their internal sense of self is sufficient foundation for identity. For many, this message feels compassionate and empowering.

Yet the burden of self-creation carries psychological weight. If the self is self-defined, then coherence depends entirely on personal certainty. Doubt becomes destabilizing. External disagreement feels threatening because it challenges the very foundation of identity.

Human beings are not designed to sustain identity in isolation. We are relational creatures. We seek affirmation, belonging, and stability. When identity must be continually asserted and defended, exhaustion follows. The expectation that others validate internal truth claims adds social pressure.

This pressure surfaces in subtle ways. Language becomes carefully monitored. Conversations are navigated cautiously. The fear of misalignment produces anxiety. Communities struggle to maintain honest dialogue without triggering perceived harm.

The desire for affirmation is not new. What is new is the belief that affirmation determines reality. If enough people affirm a claim, it is treated as true. If affirmation is withdrawn, the claim feels endangered.

This dynamic can produce fragile confidence. Public affirmation may be abundant while private uncertainty lingers. When identity is anchored externally in created reality, doubt can be addressed through reference to something stable. When identity is self-generated, doubt threatens the entire structure.

The biblical vision of identity offers relief from this pressure. To be created in the image of God is to possess dignity independent of performance or affirmation. Worth does not rise and fall with social consensus. It is secured by divine intention.

This does not eliminate struggle. It does not resolve every internal conflict. But it relocates the burden. Identity is received rather than manufactured. Truth is discovered rather than declared. The self rests within a reality larger than itself.

The psychological cost of subjective truth is rarely acknowledged in cultural debate. Attention focuses on freedom gained, not weight assumed. Yet over time, the strain becomes visible. Anxiety, polarization, and fragmentation reflect more than political disagreement. They reflect a deeper instability in how identity and authority are understood.

The question remains pressing: Can lasting human flourishing be built on self-created foundations? Or does stability require truth that exists beyond internal perception?

Truth and Human Flourishing

. . .

The debate over truth is often framed as a struggle between freedom and constraint. Subjective truth appears liberating because it promises autonomy. Revealed truth can appear restrictive because it establishes boundaries. Yet this framing may invert the deeper reality.

If truth corresponds to the way the world is actually structured, then alignment with truth is not limitation but protection. Just as physical laws govern the stability of the natural world, moral and ontological truths govern the stability of human life. Gravity is not oppressive because it restricts movement; it makes movement possible. In the same way, moral boundaries are not inherently repressive. They are formative.

The biblical narrative consistently presents truth as life-giving. Psalm 19:7 declares, "The law of the Lord is perfect, reviving the soul." Psalm 119:105 describes God's word as "a lamp to my feet and a light to my path." These metaphors suggest guidance rather than confinement. Truth illuminates; it does not imprison.

When identity is grounded in divine creation, it carries stability. A person's worth is not contingent upon social approval or internal certainty. It is rooted in being made in the image of God. That identity cannot be revoked by cultural shifts or personal doubt. It precedes achievement. It endures failure.

By contrast, when identity is self-constructed, it depends upon continual coherence between internal perception and external affirmation. If either falters, insecurity follows. The pressure to maintain alignment can produce defensiveness and fragility.

This contrast also affects community. Shared commitment to objective truth enables disagreement without dissolution. Individuals may debate interpretation while remaining anchored in common authority. When truth is subjective, disagreement threatens the foundation itself. Community becomes conditional upon affirmation.

The modern emphasis on authenticity often arises from legitimate concerns about hypocrisy and injustice. Scripture does not endorse pretense. It calls for integrity. Yet integrity in the biblical sense is alignment with reality as God has revealed it—not alignment with fluctuating perception.

Human flourishing requires more than affirmation. It requires coherence. A life built on truth that corresponds to reality possesses resilience. A life built solely on internal declaration must constantly renegotiate its foundation.

None of this denies compassion. The biblical framework commands love of neighbor, patience, and gentleness. It recognizes suffering and confusion. But love and truth are not adversaries. Ephesians 4:15 calls believers to speak "the truth in love." First Corinthians 13:6 states that love "rejoices with the truth." Compassion detached from truth becomes sentimentality. Truth detached from compassion becomes harshness. Scripture holds them together.

The cultural experiment with subjective truth is ongoing. Its appeal is powerful. It promises dignity through autonomy and freedom through self-definition. Yet it struggles to answer enduring questions: On what basis is dignity universal? Why should moral obligations bind beyond preference? How can community endure when foundational claims diverge?

The biblical worldview answers differently. Dignity is universal because it is bestowed by a Creator. Moral obligation binds because it reflects divine character. Community endures because it is grounded in shared submission to revealed truth.

The tension between these visions will not disappear quickly. It reflects competing understandings of authority and reality. But the decision each person faces is unavoidable. Either truth is something to which we conform, or it is something we construct.

If truth is constructed, then stability depends on consensus and personal conviction. If truth is revealed, then stability rests in something unchanging.

The implications reach beyond abstract theology. They shape families, churches, schools, and nations. They shape how individuals interpret suffering, pursue meaning, and understand freedom.

Chapter 1 traced the cultural fracture. Chapter 2 established the theological foundation. This chapter has explored the personal consequences of relocating truth inward. The pattern is consistent: when authority moves from revelation to perception, fragmentation follows.

The next chapter will turn specifically to the church's response. In a culture shaped by internalized authority, what does faithfulness require? How can conviction and compassion coexist? And what does it mean to stand for truth without surrendering love?

Those questions demand careful attention.

4

STANDING FIRM
WITHOUT LOSING LOVE

The church does not operate outside the cultural shifts described in the previous chapters. It lives within them. As public understanding of truth moves inward—toward self-definition and expressive identity—the church is confronted with a pressing question: How does it remain faithful to revealed truth without surrendering compassion?

This question is no longer theoretical.

In recent years, several major Christian denominations in the United States have experienced public division over questions of sexual ethics, biblical authority, and the interpretation of Scripture. The United Methodist Church, for example, has undergone widespread congregational departures following disagreements about same-sex marriage and ordination standards. These divisions were not simply about policy. They reflected deeper disagreements about whether historic doctrine is binding or subject to reinterpretation under cultural pressure.

Other denominations have faced similar internal tension. Some churches have chosen to reaffirm traditional doctrinal statements. Others have revised language in an effort to maintain broader inclusion. The divergence illustrates a larger reality: when culture redefines truth, churches must decide whether to adapt or to stand.

The pressure is not limited to denominational structures. Individual believers have encountered legal and professional conflict as well. Cases such as Masterpiece Cakeshop v. Colorado Civil Rights Commission (2018) and 303 Creative LLC v. Elenis (2023) reached the United States Supreme Court after Christian business owners declined to create custom expressive products for same-sex weddings. The legal questions involved compelled speech and religious liberty. Whatever one's political perspective, these cases demonstrate how conflicts over truth claims now extend into public commerce and conscience.

Similarly, educators and healthcare professionals in several states have faced disciplinary action or employment disputes over pronoun policies and gender-identity guidelines. In some instances, individuals have sought legal protection for conscience objections. In others, institutions have prioritized compliance with evolving regulatory interpretations. These tensions are documented, ongoing, and complex. They reveal that the debate over truth is not confined to sermons or opinion columns; it affects employment, education, and public participation.

Survey data reflects the broader shift. Research from the Cultural Research Center at Arizona Christian University has reported declining percentages of Americans who hold what researchers define as a biblical worldview. Pew Research Center studies show decreasing religious affiliation and growing numbers identifying as religiously unaffiliated. While correlation does not imply causation, these trends coincide with a cultural environment in which external authority is increasingly questioned and internal authenticity is elevated.

The church cannot ignore these realities. Yet it must also resist reacting to them with fear or hostility.

Scripture consistently joins truth and love rather than separating them. Ephesians 4:15 instructs believers to speak "the truth in love." The command assumes tension. It does not advise abandoning truth to preserve harmony, nor does it permit defending truth without compassion. The two are inseparable.

In polarized environments, however, the temptation is to choose sides in a false dichotomy. Some believers respond to cultural pressure by softening doctrinal clarity in hopes of preserving relational peace. Others respond by intensifying rhetoric, equating volume with faithfulness. Both responses are understandable. Neither fully reflects the biblical model.

The New Testament presents a different pattern. In Acts 17, the apostle Paul engages Athenian philosophers in a pluralistic setting. He begins by acknowledging their religious impulse. He quotes their poets. He reasons publicly. Yet he does not dilute his message. He proclaims that God commands repentance and has appointed a day of judgment. His engagement is respectful but clear.

Jesus Himself demonstrates the same balance. In John 8, when a woman accused of adultery is brought before Him, He prevents her public condemnation. He exposes the hypocrisy of her accusers. Yet He also tells her, "Go, and from now on sin no more." Mercy and moral clarity operate together. One does not erase the other.

In a culture that equates affirmation with love, this balance will be misunderstood. The church's refusal to redefine doctrine may be interpreted as intolerance. Its insistence on created order may be labeled regressive. But if truth is revealed and life-giving, then withholding it for the sake of social approval would not be compassionate.

At the same time, the church must examine its tone. Public discourse often rewards outrage. Social media amplifies sharp reactions and penalizes nuance. Believers are not immune to this dynamic. The temptation to respond to cultural shifts with alarmist rhetoric can distort witness. Anger may attract attention, but it rarely produces transformation.

First Peter 3:15 provides guidance for this moment: "In your hearts honor Christ the Lord as holy, always being prepared to make a defense to anyone who asks you for a reason for the hope that is in you; yet do it with gentleness and respect." Conviction and gentleness are not opposites. They are partners.

The responsibility of the church extends beyond public statements. It includes formation. Congregations must be taught not only what the Bible says, but why it says it. They must understand the theological foundations of identity, morality, and authority. Without deep grounding, cultural pressure can erode conviction gradually rather than dramatically.

This formation begins in ordinary practices: preaching that explains Scripture in context, discipleship that addresses contemporary questions honestly, community that models truth and grace, and leadership that demonstrates humility. Stability in public witness depends on clarity in private belief.

The cultural shift toward subjective truth presents a genuine challenge. It also presents an opportunity. In an environment where foundations are uncertain, a community grounded in coherent truth can offer stability rather than hostility. It can demonstrate that conviction need not produce cruelty and that compassion need not require compromise.

The question for the church is not whether it will face tension. It is whether it will navigate that tension faithfully.

The next section will explore how churches can cultivate resilience—intellectually, spiritually, and relationally—without retreating from engagement or surrendering revealed truth.

Forming Conviction in an Age of Confusion

. . .

If the church is to stand firm without losing love, it must begin with formation. Cultural resilience does not emerge from reaction; it grows from rootedness. Congregations that lack theological depth will struggle to navigate sustained pressure. Emotional intensity cannot substitute for doctrinal clarity.

The challenge many churches face today is not overt hostility but gradual drift. Cultural assumptions often enter quietly—through media, education, and everyday language—long before they are examined biblically. When believers encounter conflict later, they may feel unprepared to articulate why they hold certain convictions. Without careful formation, truth becomes fragile.

Research from the Cultural Research Center at Arizona Christian University has suggested that a declining percentage of Americans, including many who identify as Christian, consistently hold what researchers categorize as a biblical worldview. While survey methodologies can vary, the broader pattern is difficult to ignore: many churchgoers lack confidence in core doctrinal categories such as moral absolutes, the authority of Scripture, or the exclusivity of Christ.

Formation must therefore move beyond surface-level familiarity. It requires teaching believers how the biblical narrative fits together—creation, fall, redemption, and restoration. When identity debates arise, Christians must understand not only isolated verses but the larger theological arc that grounds those verses. Genesis 1–2 establishes creation order. Romans 1 describes humanity's tendency to exchange truth for self-definition. Ephesians 2 explains redemption through grace. These texts form a coherent worldview.

Pastors and leaders must also create space for honest questions. Younger generations in particular often encounter competing truth claims in educational settings and online environments. If the church responds to every question with suspicion, it risks driving sincere seekers elsewhere. Yet if it avoids clarity to preserve comfort, it fails to disciple faithfully. Patience and conviction must operate together.

Small-group discipleship can play a crucial role in this process. Large gatherings communicate vision and doctrine; smaller settings allow for dialogue and application. In such contexts, believers can wrestle with difficult questions—about identity, authority, and morality—without fear of immediate condemnation. Discipleship is not merely information transfer; it is formation of the whole person.

Church leaders must also be attentive to language. Precision matters. Terms such as "love," "justice," and "freedom" are widely used but differently defined. Without clarity, conversations quickly become confused. Careful teaching helps congregations recognize when shared vocabulary masks divergent assumptions.

Formation must extend beyond intellectual instruction to spiritual practice. Prayer, corporate worship, confession, and community accountability reinforce identity rooted in Christ rather than culture. Spiritual disciplines anchor believers in realities that do not fluctuate with public opinion. When worship centers on God's character rather than cultural commentary, perspective is restored.

Importantly, formation should cultivate humility. Standing firm does not require posturing. James 1:20 reminds believers that "the anger of man does not produce the righteousness of God." Conviction without humility hardens into pride. Humility without conviction dissolves into compromise. The church must guard against both extremes.

There is also a generational dimension to formation. Older believers often carry memory of cultural assumptions that once aligned more closely with Christian teaching. Younger believers may not share that experience. For them, the church's claims can feel countercultural from the outset. Intergenerational conversation becomes essential. Wisdom and empathy must flow both directions.

Finally, formation requires courage. Cultural approval is a powerful incentive. Churches may fear losing attendance, funding, or public reputation if they articulate unpopular truths. Yet long-term credibility depends on consistency. If doctrine shifts with every cultural wave, trust erodes internally even if tension temporarily decreases externally.

Courage, however, is not combative. It is steady. It is the quiet refusal to detach conviction from compassion. It recognizes that faithfulness is measured not by applause but by alignment with revealed truth.

The cultural moment demands more than reaction. It demands rooted communities capable of articulating why truth matters—and demonstrating through lived example that truth and love are not adversaries.

Speaking Clearly in Public Spaces

Formation within the church must translate into thoughtful engagement beyond it. Public witness is inevitable. The question is whether that witness will be characterized by clarity and respect or by confusion and hostility.

Believers today often find themselves navigating conversations in workplaces, schools, and online platforms where truth claims are contested. The instinct may be either to withdraw entirely or to engage aggressively. Scripture suggests a third path.

Colossians 4:6 instructs, "Let your speech always be gracious, seasoned with salt, so that you may know how you ought to answer each person." Gracious speech does not mean evasive speech. It means measured, thoughtful, and anchored in truth.

When engaging contentious topics, Christians benefit from distinguishing between explanation and condemnation. Explaining why one holds a conviction invites dialogue. Condemnation shuts it down. The difference is not merely rhetorical; it reflects posture.

It is also important to recognize legal and civic realities accurately. Religious liberty protections in the United States, for example, are grounded in constitutional principles that continue to be interpreted through the courts. Supreme Court decisions such as Masterpiece Cakeshop and 303 Creative addressed specific questions about compelled speech and free exercise. They did not resolve every future dispute. Responsible engagement requires understanding both rights and limits.

Clear public witness also avoids exaggeration. Cultural shifts are real, but apocalyptic framing can distort credibility. When Christians overstate threats, they risk undermining their own message. Accuracy strengthens trust.

At the same time, silence is not neutrality. If truth is revealed and life-giving, withholding it from public discourse leaves cultural narratives unchallenged. The aim is not dominance but presence—faithful presence that speaks without coercion and listens without surrender.

Public engagement must be sustained by prayer and grounded in community. Individuals standing alone can become reactive or discouraged. A church rooted in shared conviction provides account-ability and support.

The balance is demanding. It requires theological clarity, emotional maturity, and spiritual dependence. Yet this balance reflects the char-acter of Christ, who embodied both grace and truth (John 1:14).

Guarding Against Reaction and Retreat

In moments of cultural tension, churches are tempted toward two opposite errors: reaction and retreat. Reaction manifests as alarmism, anger, and a posture of perpetual grievance. Retreat appears as silence, ambiguity, and gradual doctrinal erosion. Both may feel understandable. Neither produces long-term faithfulness.

Reaction often arises from fear. Rapid social change can feel destabi-lizing, particularly for congregations that remember cultural assump-tions once aligned more closely with Christian teaching. Yet fear-driven rhetoric can distort witness. When public communication is dominated by outrage, it reinforces the perception that conviction requires hostility.

The New Testament offers a different pattern. Second Timothy 1:7 reminds believers that "God gave us a spirit not of fear but of power and love and self-control." Power without love becomes coercion. Love without self-control becomes sentimentality. Self-control without conviction becomes passivity. The biblical posture integrates all three.

Retreat, by contrast, is subtler. It may begin with a desire to avoid unnecessary offense. Over time, however, it can produce doctrinal vagueness. Churches may stop addressing controversial topics altogether. Teaching becomes selective. Language grows increasingly abstract. The result is not peace but confusion.

Historical examples illustrate the risk of accommodation. In various periods of church history, movements that attempted to align doctrine entirely with prevailing cultural philosophies eventually lost theological distinctiveness. While cultural engagement is necessary, wholesale adaptation dissolves identity.

The challenge is to maintain theological clarity without collapsing into culture war. This requires distinguishing between conviction and partisanship. Not every moral issue is reducible to political alignment. When churches appear indistinguishable from political platforms, their spiritual authority weakens.

Pastoral Care in Contested Spaces

The practical implications of these tensions are felt most acutely at the pastoral level. Real people bring real questions into church offices and living rooms. Conversations about identity, sexuality, conscience, and doubt are not abstract debates; they involve family members, long-standing friendships, and personal struggle.

Pastoral care must begin with listening. James 1:19 urges believers to be "quick to hear, slow to speak, slow to anger." Listening does not imply agreement. It communicates dignity. Many individuals navigating identity questions carry experiences of confusion, rejection, or internal conflict. Dismissing those experiences prematurely closes the door to meaningful guidance.

At the same time, pastoral care cannot detach from biblical conviction. Compassion that affirms every self-perception as truth may feel kind in the moment but risks reinforcing instability. The church must offer something deeper than affirmation—it must offer direction rooted in created order and redemption.

Concrete examples help clarify this balance. In recent years, some churches have developed pastoral guidelines addressing how to walk with individuals experiencing gender dysphoria or same-sex attraction without abandoning doctrinal convictions. These guidelines often emphasize hospitality, confidentiality, and long-term discipleship while maintaining historic teaching on sexuality. They illustrate that pastoral care and doctrinal clarity are not mutually exclusive.

Similarly, parents within congregations increasingly seek guidance on how to speak with children and teenagers encountering identity frameworks in school or online. Churches that proactively equip families—through seminars, small groups, and counseling resources—demonstrate care without panic. Proactivity prevents reaction.

It is also important to recognize that disagreement within congregations will occur. Members may differ in how they interpret cultural developments or legal decisions. Leaders must cultivate environments where secondary disagreements do not fracture fellowship. Romans 14 provides wisdom for navigating disputable matters while preserving unity around core doctrine.

Compassion Without Compromise

. . .

Perhaps the most difficult task for the church in this cultural moment is demonstrating that compassion and conviction are not enemies. Cultural narratives often portray them as opposites: one must choose between kindness and truth. Scripture refuses this dichotomy.

Jesus embodies both. John 1:14 describes Him as "full of grace and truth." Grace without truth would have ignored sin. Truth without grace would have crushed sinners. The incarnation reveals that the two are inseparable.

Compassion without compromise requires emotional maturity. It requires patience when conversations move slowly. It requires resisting caricatures. It requires acknowledging that some objections to Christianity arise from genuine pain rather than ideological hostility.

At the same time, compromise disguised as compassion ultimately undermines hope. If the church abandons its conviction that truth corresponds to created reality, it offers little more than cultural affirmation. The distinctiveness of the gospel lies precisely in its claim that reality is grounded in a personal, holy Creator who redeems and restores.

This does not mean every public controversy requires a pulpit response. Wisdom discerns timing. Not every headline deserves immediate commentary. Churches that tether their preaching schedule to news cycles risk becoming reactive rather than rooted.

Instead, steady exposition of Scripture builds resilience. When believers are consistently taught how the Bible addresses identity, morality, suffering, and redemption, they are less likely to be destabilized by each new cultural development.

The ultimate goal is not cultural dominance but faithful presence. The church's mission remains unchanged: proclaim Christ, disciple believers, and embody love grounded in truth. Cultural conditions may shift, but calling does not.

As public definitions of truth continue to evolve, the church will face ongoing tension. Yet tension does not equal defeat. Throughout history, Christian communities have flourished under pressure when anchored in conviction and animated by love.

The final section of this chapter will draw these threads together and consider how sustained faithfulness shapes long-term witness.

A Faithful Presence in a Shifting Culture

The cultural movement toward internalized truth is unlikely to reverse quickly. Generational change, technological acceleration, and institutional realignment continue to reinforce expressive individualism. Churches should not expect cultural stability as a prerequisite for faithfulness. Stability has never been the foundation of Christian witness.

What the church must recover is not cultural influence but theological confidence. Confidence does not mean arrogance. It means settled conviction that truth is not self-created but revealed, and that revelation is not oppressive but life-giving.

Throughout church history, Christian communities have navigated environments far more hostile than the present moment. The early church grew within an empire that did not share its moral framework. Believers were misunderstood, misrepresented, and at times persecuted. Yet their witness was marked by both clarity and care. They rescued abandoned infants, tended to the sick during plagues, and maintained moral distinctiveness in a culture that did not affirm it.

Their strength did not come from majority approval. It came from rooted identity.

In the same way, the church today must resist measuring success by cultural applause. Faithfulness is not determined by trending approval or online affirmation. It is measured by alignment with Scripture and the fruit of transformed lives.

This does not mean disengagement from public life. Christians are called to be "salt and light" (Matthew 5:13–16). Salt preserves. Light reveals. Neither withdraws. Both influence quietly but consistently.

Faithful presence involves several commitments.

First, the church must continue teaching the whole counsel of God. Selective silence creates theological imbalance. Difficult passages cannot be avoided simply because they provoke controversy. At the same time, preaching must reflect the full biblical narrative—sin and redemption, judgment and mercy, truth and grace.

Second, churches must cultivate durable community. In a culture where identity is increasingly self-defined and isolated, the local church offers embodied belonging. Shared worship, shared service, and shared accountability counteract fragmentation. Believers who are deeply known and loved are less likely to experience disagreement as abandonment.

Third, the church must model civil discourse. When cultural debate becomes harsh, Christians should not mirror the tone. Civility is not weakness; it is discipline. It reflects confidence that truth does not require coercion. The apostle Paul writes in 2 Corinthians 10:5 that believers "take every thought captive to obey Christ." The metaphor is intellectual, not violent. Ideas are engaged thoughtfully.

Fourth, the church must prepare believers for cost. In environments where historic Christian doctrine conflicts with prevailing norms, there may be social or professional consequences. Jesus Himself warned that following Him would involve difficulty (John 16:33). Preparing believers honestly prevents disillusionment.

Cost, however, does not negate hope. The gospel proclaims restoration. It offers forgiveness for sin, healing for brokenness, and reconciliation with God. It addresses the deepest human needs—identity, meaning, belonging—not by encouraging self-construction but by inviting surrender to divine grace.

The tension between subjective and revealed truth ultimately concerns authority. Either the self is ultimate, or God is. This is not a new conflict. From Genesis 3 onward, humanity has wrestled with the temptation to define good and evil independently. The question remains unchanged: Will we trust the Creator, or will we assert autonomy?

The church's task is not to win every cultural argument. It is to remain faithful to revelation and to embody that revelation with humility. Conviction anchored in love is persuasive over time. Hostility rarely is.

Cultural climates shift. Legal frameworks evolve. Social consensus fluctuates. The character of God does not. Malachi 3:6 declares, "For I the Lord do not change." That stability provides confidence amid volatility.

When believers stand firmly yet speak gently, they reflect the pattern of Christ. When they care for those who disagree with them, they demonstrate that love is not dependent on affirmation. When they refuse to redefine truth to avoid discomfort, they testify that reality is not determined by consensus.

The future of the church will not be secured by strategy alone. It will be sustained by faithfulness—faithfulness in teaching, in discipleship, in pastoral care, and in public engagement.

The chapters ahead will explore what it means to recover courage rooted in conviction and humility rooted in grace. If truth is not self-defined, then it must be rediscovered and reembraced—not as a weapon, but as a foundation.

Only on such a foundation can love endure.

5

WHEN A NATION LOSES
ITS MORAL CENTER

Nations do not collapse overnight. They drift. The drift is rarely announced. It begins with small shifts in language, then in law, then in assumption. Over time, what once seemed fixed becomes negotiable. What once seemed self-evident becomes controversial.

The question of truth is not merely personal or ecclesial. It is civilizational.

Every society operates with underlying moral assumptions. Laws do not emerge from neutrality. They reflect judgments about justice, dignity, responsibility, and harm. Even pluralistic democracies require some shared understanding of what is good and what is binding. Without that shared moral center, coherence weakens.

Historically, the American experiment was shaped by a moral framework influenced significantly by biblical concepts. The language of inherent rights, human dignity, and equality under law did not emerge in a vacuum. The Declaration of Independence grounds rights in a Creator. Whether every citizen shared theological conviction is beside the point; the public vocabulary assumed transcendence.

Over time, however, public discourse has shifted. Appeals to divine authority have increasingly been replaced with appeals to autonomy or consensus. Rights are often framed as expressions of self-definition rather than recognition of created order. The moral center moves from transcendent grounding to internal assertion.

This shift carries consequences.

If rights originate in a Creator, they are inherent and universal. If they originate in collective agreement, they can be revised. If dignity is bestowed by God, it remains stable regardless of political climate. If dignity is conferred by society, it depends on prevailing sentiment.

These distinctions may appear philosophical, but they shape policy debates. Questions about life, marriage, education, speech, and conscience all assume underlying definitions of personhood and authority. When those definitions diverge, public conflict intensifies.

Recent decades have seen increasing polarization around such questions. Legislative debates over religious liberty, gender identity policy, and parental authority reflect deeper disagreements about truth and human nature. These disputes are often framed politically, yet beneath the partisanship lies a more foundational fracture: What is real, and who decides?

Trust in institutions has declined across ideological lines. Surveys from Pew Research Center and Gallup over the past decade have documented decreasing confidence in government, media, and other civic institutions. While multiple factors contribute to this decline, fragmentation of shared moral assumptions plays a role. When citizens no longer agree on foundational truths, institutional trust becomes difficult to sustain.

A nation does not require theological uniformity to function. It does require some shared moral grammar. Without it, law becomes an instrument of power rather than reflection of justice. Public discourse shifts from persuasion to coercion.

The erosion of shared truth also affects civic friendship. Democracy depends not only on elections but on mutual recognition of legitimacy. When opposing viewpoints are treated not merely as mistaken but as illegitimate or dangerous, civil society strains. Disagreement becomes existential.

History provides sobering reminders. Societies that sever moral reasoning from transcendent grounding often struggle to sustain coherence over time. While contexts differ and historical comparisons must be handled carefully, the pattern of moral drift preceding institutional instability is well documented in various civilizations.

This does not mean decline is inevitable. It does mean drift has direction.

The present cultural moment is marked by extraordinary technological advancement, economic complexity, and global interconnection. Yet beneath these strengths lies a question that cannot be solved by innovation alone: What anchors us?

If truth is primarily self-defined, then national cohesion depends on negotiated consensus among competing identities. If truth is revealed and stable, cohesion rests on recognition of realities beyond preference.

The future of any nation is shaped not only by policy but by moral imagination. What do its citizens believe about human nature? About authority? About accountability? About freedom?

Freedom itself is redefined when truth shifts. Is freedom the absence of constraint, or the ability to live in alignment with reality? If the former, then law becomes a necessary limitation of competing desires. If the latter, then law can function as a guide toward flourishing.

The debate is not abstract. It surfaces in classrooms, courtrooms, legislatures, and homes. It surfaces in the way children are taught about identity, in the way rights are articulated, and in the way disagreement is handled.

A nation that loses confidence in objective truth may continue to function materially for some time. Economic systems can persist even amid moral confusion. But over generations, the erosion of shared truth reshapes culture from within.

The question, then, is not whether cultural change is occurring. It clearly is. The question is whether renewal is possible.

Moments of Moral and Spiritual Renewal

History demonstrates that moral drift is not irreversible. Periods of decline have, at times, been followed by renewal. These renewals rarely begin in legislatures. They begin in hearts, congregations, and communities.

In the eighteenth century, the First Great Awakening swept through the American colonies. Preachers such as Jonathan Edwards and George Whitefield emphasized repentance, personal conversion, and the authority of Scripture. While historians continue to debate the precise political implications of the movement, there is broad agreement that it reshaped religious life and reinvigorated church participation across multiple denominations.

The Second Great Awakening in the early nineteenth century similarly produced widespread religious revival. Camp meetings and renewed preaching emphasized personal responsibility before God. Out of that revival emerged reform movements addressing issues such as abolition, temperance, and prison reform. The connection between spiritual renewal and social reform was not accidental. Moral transformation at the individual level often spilled into public concern for justice.

These awakenings were not perfect. They were marked by excesses, theological disagreements, and uneven outcomes. Yet they illustrate an enduring pattern: when truth is proclaimed clearly and repentance is embraced sincerely, cultural impact can follow.

Renewal is not uniquely American, nor is it confined to a single tradition. Across history, movements of repentance and reform have emerged in diverse contexts. The Protestant Reformation in sixteenth-century Europe reshaped theology, church structure, and eventually political life. In England, the evangelical revivals associated with John Wesley and others contributed to social reform movements that addressed labor conditions and education.

These examples should not be romanticized. Societies remain complex and imperfect even after revival. But they demonstrate that cultural trajectories are not fixed. Spiritual conviction can influence public life.

Scripture presents similar patterns. In the Old Testament, seasons of national drift were often followed by calls to repentance. The reforms under King Josiah in 2 Kings 22–23 began with rediscovery of the Book of the Law. Upon hearing its words, Josiah tore his garments in repentance and initiated covenant renewal. The reform did not erase prior corruption, but it marked a decisive return to revealed truth.

In the New Testament, the spread of the gospel transformed communities within the Roman Empire. Acts 19 records that in Ephesus, many who practiced magic publicly burned their scrolls after embracing the faith. The text notes that the value of the scrolls was substantial. Conversion carried social and economic consequences.

Renewal, therefore, is not merely emotional enthusiasm. It involves realignment with truth. It includes repentance, restitution, and reformation of habits. It alters both personal behavior and communal norms.

Modern societies differ from ancient Israel or colonial America. Legal structures, pluralism, and global interdependence complicate direct comparison. Yet the underlying principle remains consistent: moral and spiritual renewal begins with recognition that truth exists beyond the self.

Contemporary data suggests both challenge and opportunity. While affiliation with organized religion has declined in many Western contexts, surveys also indicate persistent spiritual curiosity. Many individuals express dissatisfaction with purely material explanations of meaning. Anxiety, loneliness, and polarization have prompted renewed conversation about purpose and belonging.

These indicators do not guarantee revival. They do suggest that moral vacuum does not eliminate longing. When shared frameworks weaken, the hunger for coherence often intensifies.

The path toward renewal cannot be engineered mechanically. It cannot be legislated into existence. It requires proclamation of truth, humble repentance, and patient discipleship. It requires churches willing to speak clearly without rancor and to serve communities without demanding control.

Renewal also demands self-examination. Cultural critique is easier than personal confession. Yet throughout Scripture, calls to national restoration begin with the people of God. Second Chronicles 7:14 records the familiar promise: "If my people who are called by my name humble themselves, and pray and seek my face and turn from their wicked ways, then I will hear from heaven." While the verse was addressed to ancient Israel, the principle of humility preceding restoration remains instructive.

A nation's moral center is strengthened when its citizens recover shared commitments to truth and responsibility. Political systems may reflect that recovery, but they rarely initiate it.

The question for this generation is not simply whether cultural trends are troubling. It is whether individuals and communities are willing to return to foundations that transcend preference.

Obstacles to Renewal in a Polarized Age

If renewal is possible, it is not inevitable. Cultural drift does not automatically produce repentance. In fact, certain conditions make renewal more difficult.

One significant obstacle is polarization. In highly divided environments, moral questions are quickly absorbed into partisan identity. Issues of conscience become markers of political allegiance. When truth claims are interpreted primarily through party alignment, spiritual reflection is overshadowed by ideological loyalty.

This dynamic affects public discourse. Individuals may hesitate to reconsider positions not because evidence is lacking, but because doing so would feel like betraying a political tribe. Convictions harden. Dialogue narrows. The search for truth is replaced by defense of affiliation.

Media ecosystems amplify this fragmentation. The modern information landscape rewards speed and emotional intensity. Outrage travels faster than nuance. Headlines are often crafted to provoke reaction rather than reflection. In such an environment, careful moral reasoning struggles to compete with immediacy.

Social media compounds the challenge. Algorithms curate content aligned with prior preferences, reinforcing existing beliefs. Exposure to opposing perspectives may occur, but often in caricatured form. The result is mutual suspicion rather than shared understanding.

Cynicism also presents a barrier. When trust in institutions declines, appeals to moral reform may be dismissed as naïve or manipulative. Scandals involving religious leaders have, at times, further eroded confidence. Calls for repentance can sound hollow if not accompanied by integrity.

Economic and technological complexity adds another layer. Modern life is fast-paced and fragmented. Many individuals experience constant distraction. Sustained reflection on moral foundations requires attention that is increasingly scarce. Renewal demands depth in a culture that prizes immediacy.

There is also the obstacle of comfort. Moral drift does not always produce visible crisis in the short term. Societies can function economically and technologically even while foundational assumptions shift. Without immediate collapse, urgency fades. Convenience dulls concern.

Yet Scripture consistently portrays renewal as beginning with clarity rather than panic. In Nehemiah 8, when Ezra read the Book of the Law publicly, the people wept as they recognized how far they had departed from its instruction. Their response was not orchestrated hysteria but sober recognition.

Renewal requires similar honesty. It requires acknowledging where truth has been neglected—personally and collectively. It requires humility rather than self-righteousness.

Another obstacle is the fear of social cost. In environments where adherence to traditional moral claims may invite criticism or professional consequence, silence can feel safer. Fear discourages public conviction. Yet fear also perpetuates drift.

At the same time, boldness without wisdom can be counterproductive. Renewal is not achieved through volume. It is sustained through consistency. Faithfulness expressed steadily over time often has more impact than momentary confrontation.

Importantly, obstacles to renewal are not solely external. Internal fragmentation within churches can weaken witness. When congregations are divided by political rhetoric or distracted by secondary disputes, their ability to model coherent truth diminishes.

The path forward therefore requires recalibration. It requires disentangling core theological commitments from partisan identity. It requires refusing to mirror the hostility of the surrounding culture. It requires recovering moral imagination rooted in something deeper than reaction.

From National Concern to Personal Responsibility

It is tempting to speak of national renewal in sweeping terms. Yet nations are composed of individuals. Cultural transformation begins not with abstract rhetoric but with personal conviction.

Scripture consistently moves from collective diagnosis to individual response. The prophets addressed nations, but they called individuals to repentance. Jesus preached to crowds, but He invited personal faith. Cultural concern without personal examination becomes abstraction.

If truth has eroded at the national level, it has done so through countless personal decisions—decisions to remain silent, to compromise gradually, to disengage, or to redefine convictions to align with comfort. Renewal must therefore begin with different decisions.

Personal responsibility includes intellectual honesty. It requires examining whether one's beliefs are grounded in revealed truth or shaped primarily by cultural assumption. It requires willingness to submit preferences to Scripture rather than reshaping Scripture to match preference.

It also includes relational courage. Conversations about truth are often uncomfortable. Yet respectful dialogue is essential. Avoiding disagreement entirely may preserve surface peace while allowing deeper confusion to grow.

Communities matter as well. Individual conviction is strengthened within shared commitment. When believers gather for worship, study, and service, they reinforce a worldview that transcends individual perception. Renewal spreads through networks of faithful communities rather than isolated voices.

National trends can feel overwhelming. But renewal has rarely begun with majority consensus. It often starts with small groups committed to truth and integrity. Over time, their influence expands not through coercion but through example.

. . .

Hope Beyond Drift

Cultural drift can feel disorienting, particularly when viewed at a national scale. Yet history and Scripture both remind us that decline is not destiny. The future of a nation is shaped not only by trends but by convictions lived out over time.

Hope does not begin with denial of difficulty. It begins with clarity. A society that recognizes its moral confusion has taken a first step toward correction. The danger lies not in disagreement but in indifference. When citizens cease to care about truth altogether, renewal becomes unlikely. When concern remains, possibility endures.

The path forward will not be uniform or immediate. Political cycles will continue. Court decisions will evolve. Cultural debates will intensify and then shift. These fluctuations, while significant, are not ultimate. The deeper question concerns formation: What beliefs are being transmitted to the next generation?

Generational transmission is often overlooked in national analysis. Laws matter. Elections matter. But families, schools, and churches shape moral imagination more enduringly than headlines. Children absorb assumptions about identity, authority, and responsibility long before they can articulate them.

If truth is treated as fluid within formative environments, it will feel fluid in adulthood. If it is treated as stable and life-giving, it will carry weight beyond adolescence. The work of renewal, therefore, is patient. It invests in teaching, modeling, and mentoring.

Scripture consistently emphasizes generational faithfulness. Deuteronomy 6 instructs parents to speak of God's commandments "when you sit in your house, and when you walk by the way, and when you lie down, and when you rise." Truth is not merely proclaimed publicly; it is woven into daily life.

National health is inseparable from personal integrity. Citizens who value honesty, responsibility, and self-restraint contribute to stable civic life. When these virtues erode, no system can compensate indefinitely. Renewal at scale reflects renewal at the level of character.

This does not imply nostalgia for an imagined golden age. Every era contains its own failures and blind spots. The goal is not restoration of a particular cultural moment but recovery of foundational truth. That truth transcends political cycles and cultural fashions.

Hope also requires patience. Quick fixes are attractive, but durable change unfolds gradually. The early Christians did not transform the Roman Empire through immediate policy shifts. They bore witness steadily, cared for the vulnerable, and formed resilient communities. Over time, their convictions reshaped cultural norms.

In the same way, contemporary renewal will likely appear incremental. It may begin in congregations committed to faithful teaching. It may emerge in families that prioritize Scripture and prayer. It may grow through individuals who refuse to separate truth from compassion in public engagement.

The obstacles described earlier—polarization, cynicism, distraction —are real. Yet they are not insurmountable. Clarity counters confusion. Integrity counters cynicism. Discipline counters distraction. Courage counters fear.

Ultimately, the question returns to authority. If truth is revealed and enduring, then it remains available for rediscovery. It does not disappear because it is ignored. It waits to be recognized.

A nation's moral center is strengthened when enough citizens recover confidence in realities that transcend preference. Such confidence does not produce uniformity, but it provides common ground. It allows disagreement without dissolution and diversity without fragmentation.

The church plays a crucial role in this process, but it does not act alone. Believers carry conviction into workplaces, schools, civic institutions, and neighborhoods. Faithfulness expressed consistently in ordinary contexts shapes culture more deeply than episodic controversy.

Hope, therefore, is not naïve optimism. It is grounded expectation that truth, when lived and proclaimed with humility, retains transformative power. The question is whether individuals and communities will choose alignment over accommodation.

The chapters ahead will turn from national perspective to practical application—what courage looks like in everyday life, and how conviction rooted in grace can withstand cultural pressure without surrendering love.

Drift is real. So is renewal.

The direction depends on what we choose to anchor.

6

COURAGE IN ORDINARY FAITHFULNESS

Cultural change often feels overwhelming because it appears to operate at scale. Laws shift. Institutions realign. Language evolves. Headlines intensify. The temptation is to respond at the same scale—to think that only national strategies or sweeping reform movements can make a difference.

Yet Scripture consistently locates faithfulness at a smaller level.

Before cultures change, individuals choose.

Before institutions shift, convictions form.

Before nations renew, people stand.

The question facing believers in this moment is not first, "How do we fix the culture?" It is, "Will I remain faithful?"

Courage in this sense is not dramatic. It is not loud. It is rarely viral. It is the steady refusal to detach conviction from conduct.

The modern environment places subtle pressure on that steadiness. The pressure does not always arrive through persecution. Often it arrives through normalization. Ideas that once felt controversial gradually become assumed. Practices once debated become routine. The cost of dissent becomes social rather than legal—strained relationships, professional tension, reputational risk.

For many Christians, the pressure is not to renounce faith but to privatize it. Belief is acceptable as long as it remains internal and non-disruptive. Public alignment with revealed truth, particularly in contested areas, can invite scrutiny. The expectation is not hostility but accommodation.

This is where courage becomes necessary.

Courage, biblically understood, is not aggression. It is fidelity under pressure. In Joshua 1:9, the command to "be strong and courageous" is not paired with conquest rhetoric but with obedience: "Be careful to do according to all the law." Strength and courage are linked to alignment with God's instruction.

Ordinary faithfulness requires that same alignment.

It means telling the truth when ambiguity would be easier.

It means declining to participate in speech that contradicts conviction.

It means maintaining integrity in environments that reward compromise.

It means refusing caricature, even when caricature is directed at you.

The cost may be modest in some contexts and significant in others. Not every believer will face public controversy. Many will simply navigate quiet tension—moments in workplaces or classrooms when silence would protect comfort but speech would reflect conviction.

The New Testament anticipates such tension. First Peter addresses believers scattered across a pluralistic society. They were not political power brokers. They were minorities navigating cultural distance. Peter does not instruct them to withdraw. He calls them to live "honorably among the Gentiles" (1 Peter 2:12), to endure suffering if necessary, and to respond with gentleness and respect.

The model is not triumph but endurance.

Endurance differs from reaction. Reaction is immediate and emotional. Endurance is steady and disciplined. Reaction often seeks immediate resolution. Endurance trusts that faithfulness over time bears fruit.

In a polarized age, reaction is rewarded. Outrage travels quickly. Calm conviction rarely trends. Yet long-term credibility is built not through spikes of attention but through patterns of integrity.

Courage in ordinary faithfulness also requires internal clarity. It is difficult to stand for truth one has not carefully considered. Many believers inherit convictions without examining their foundations. When challenged, uncertainty can surface. The solution is not defensiveness but depth.

Depth grows through disciplined engagement with Scripture, thoughtful study, and conversation within trusted community. Leaders and pastors play a crucial role in cultivating such depth, but individual responsibility remains. A borrowed conviction may sustain briefly; a tested conviction endures.

Courage also requires humility. Standing firm does not mean assuming moral superiority. It means recognizing that one's confidence rests not in personal righteousness but in revealed truth. The believer stands not because he is better, but because he believes something beyond himself.

This humility guards against harshness. It prevents conviction from curdling into contempt. It allows disagreement without dehumanization.

In practical terms, ordinary faithfulness often looks unspectacular. It is a parent speaking clearly with a child about identity and dignity. It is an employee respectfully declining participation in speech that violates conscience. It is a pastor teaching difficult passages without softening their meaning. It is a student engaging discussion without surrendering conviction.

None of these acts may alter national headlines. Yet multiplied across communities, they shape culture from within.

The erosion of shared truth described in earlier chapters did not occur overnight. It emerged from countless incremental shifts—small accommodations, quiet redefinitions, gradual silences. In the same way, renewal rarely begins with dramatic spectacle. It begins with individuals choosing consistency over comfort.

Courage in ordinary faithfulness is therefore foundational. Without it, discussions of institutional rebuilding remain abstract. With it, cultural influence becomes organic rather than engineered.

Faithfulness in Family

If cultural drift unfolds gradually, renewal begins just as gradually—often in homes long before it appears in institutions. Families are primary sites of moral formation. They transmit assumptions about truth, authority, and identity through daily habits rather than public statements.

In a culture where truth is frequently framed as self-defined, children absorb powerful counter-messages before they reach adulthood. Media, education, and peer environments all contribute to shaping moral imagination. Parents cannot control every influence, but they can cultivate clarity.

Faithfulness in family life begins with conversation. Silence leaves interpretation to surrounding voices. Clarity, offered calmly and consistently, builds resilience. When children understand why their family holds certain convictions—rather than merely knowing that it does—they are better equipped to navigate competing claims.

This requires patience. Cultural questions often surface earlier than previous generations expected. Discussions about identity, dignity, sexuality, and responsibility may arise in elementary settings rather than adolescence. Parents who respond with composure rather than alarm create space for thoughtful engagement.

Modeling matters as much as instruction. Children observe how adults handle disagreement, stress, and moral tension. If conviction is expressed with hostility, they may associate truth with anger. If it is expressed with steadiness and kindness, they learn that clarity and compassion can coexist.

Faithfulness in family also involves accountability. Boundaries, when explained within the larger story of creation and redemption, feel purposeful rather than arbitrary. Discipline grounded in love communicates that moral order protects flourishing.

The long-term effect of such formation is cumulative. Cultural trends may fluctuate, but a household anchored in coherent truth provides stability that extends into adulthood. Generational transmission is rarely dramatic; it is consistent.

Faithfulness in Vocation

For many believers, the workplace represents the most immediate arena of tension. Professional environments increasingly reflect evolving norms about language, identity, and moral expectation. Navigating these spaces requires discernment.

Faithfulness in vocation does not require constant confrontation. It requires integrity. An employee who performs work diligently, treats colleagues respectfully, and communicates honestly embodies conviction even before speaking explicitly about belief.

At times, however, speech becomes necessary. Policies or expectations may arise that conflict with conscience. In such moments, the manner of response matters. Clear explanation, delivered respectfully and without accusation, preserves credibility even when disagreement remains.

Legal frameworks in many democratic societies continue to recognize some degree of conscience protection. Yet even where legal protection exists, social cost may follow. Courage, therefore, must be paired with wisdom. Not every disagreement requires public escalation. Some require quiet clarification. Others require principled refusal.

Leaders, in particular, carry added responsibility. Pastors, educators, executives, and civic officials shape institutional tone. Their steadiness influences others. When leaders respond to cultural tension with panic or hostility, they transmit instability. When they respond with clarity and composure, they cultivate confidence.

Faithfulness in vocation also includes resisting subtle compromise. It may be tempting to adopt ambiguous language that obscures conviction in order to avoid discomfort. Over time, such ambiguity erodes coherence. Precision, even when costly, sustains integrity.

Faithfulness in Public Speech

Public discourse has become increasingly reactive. Digital platforms reward immediacy and emotional intensity. In such an environment, measured speech can appear weak. Yet Scripture consistently links wisdom with restraint.

James 3 warns of the power of the tongue. Words shape perception. They build or fracture trust. Believers committed to truth must also commit to discipline in speech.

Faithfulness in public speech involves several practices. First, accuracy. Exaggeration undermines credibility. If cultural concerns are overstated, thoughtful listeners disengage. Second, charity. Representing opposing views fairly strengthens argument. Third, consistency. A pattern of respectful engagement over time carries more weight than isolated moments of confrontation.

Silence can sometimes be prudent. Not every controversy requires immediate comment. Discernment distinguishes between issues central to conviction and those peripheral. When believers speak selectively rather than reflexively, their words carry greater authority.

At the same time, habitual silence in the face of clear moral confusion communicates uncertainty. Courage does not seek attention, but it does refuse evasion when truth is at stake.

Public faithfulness must therefore balance clarity and restraint. The aim is not dominance but witness. The believer speaks not to win every exchange but to remain aligned with revealed truth.

The cumulative effect of such steadiness is often underestimated. Cultural environments may appear volatile, but consistent integrity influences quietly. Families observe it. Colleagues notice it. Congregations learn from it.

Ordinary faithfulness, lived across spheres of life, becomes the seedbed of long-term cultural health.

Endurance Over Outrage

The defining temptation of the present cultural moment is not only compromise. It is outrage.

Outrage is powerful because it feels righteous. It offers immediate clarity in a confusing environment. It creates solidarity among those who agree. It rewards visible intensity. In digital spaces especially, outrage travels quickly and is often mistaken for courage.

Yet outrage and courage are not the same.

Outrage reacts.

Courage endures.

Outrage seeks immediate resolution.

Courage accepts long obedience.

Scripture consistently favors endurance over reaction. Hebrews 12:1 calls believers to "run with endurance the race that is set before us." The metaphor is not explosive; it is sustained. The Christian life is portrayed not as a series of emotional spikes but as a steady pursuit of faithfulness.

In polarized environments, emotional escalation is contagious. When one side raises its voice, the other feels pressure to match the volume. The result is a cycle of amplification. Nuance disappears. Trust erodes. Witness suffers.

The church must resist this cycle.

Endurance does not mean passivity. It means disciplined steadiness. It means refusing to allow external volatility to dictate internal posture. It means maintaining composure when provoked and clarity when pressured.

Practically, this requires self-examination. Why do certain issues provoke immediate anger? Is the reaction rooted in conviction or in fear? Fear of cultural loss can produce defensive aggression. Conviction rooted in truth produces patient clarity.

Second Timothy 2:24–25 provides an instructive model: "The Lord's servant must not be quarrelsome but kind to everyone, able to teach, patiently enduring evil, correcting his opponents with gentleness." Notice the pairing: correction and gentleness, endurance and instruction. Truth is not abandoned; it is delivered without hostility.

Endurance also requires a long view of history. Cultural movements rarely reverse quickly. Legislation shifts. Social norms fluctuate. Yet over decades, patient communities shape imagination more effectively than reactive bursts of attention.

Consider the early church once more. It operated in a society that did not affirm its moral framework. It lacked political leverage. It possessed no media platform. Yet through consistent proclamation, sacrificial care for the vulnerable, and durable community life, it reshaped cultural assumptions gradually.

The temptation today is to seek immediate cultural restoration. Yet the pattern of Scripture suggests something different: sustained faithfulness over time.

This long view reshapes practical life.

In families, endurance means teaching patiently even when children question inherited convictions. It means answering objections without panic and modeling integrity even when cultural messaging intensifies.

In vocation, endurance means maintaining ethical consistency even when shortcuts promise advancement. It means continuing excellent work even when recognition is withheld because of conviction.

In public speech, endurance means resisting the urge to respond instantly to every controversy. It means choosing words carefully, accepting misunderstanding when necessary, and trusting that credibility grows through repetition of character.

Theologically, endurance rests on confidence in the unchanging character of God. Malachi 3:6 declares, "For I the Lord do not change." Cultural frameworks fluctuate, but divine reality remains constant. Courage flows from this stability. If truth is grounded in God rather than in consensus, then it is not threatened by temporary unpopularity.

Endurance also protects against despair. When cultural shifts feel relentless, discouragement can follow. The belief that everything is collapsing breeds either panic or apathy. Scripture counters both. In Galatians 6:9, believers are exhorted not to "grow weary of doing good, for in due season we will reap, if we do not give up." The promise is not immediate harvest but eventual fruit.

This perspective reframes cultural engagement. The goal is not to win every argument but to remain faithful across seasons. Influence that emerges from endurance is more durable than influence driven by reaction.

There is, however, a cost. Endurance can be misunderstood as weakness. Calm conviction may be interpreted as indifference. The refusal to escalate may frustrate those who equate passion with intensity. Yet Scripture repeatedly affirms that strength is often quiet. Proverbs 16:32 observes, "Whoever is slow to anger is better than the mighty." Self-control is portrayed as strength, not timidity.

For leaders and pastors, this principle is especially critical. Congregations absorb tone. If leaders embody outrage, congregations mirror it. If leaders model steadiness, congregations learn restraint. Over time, this shapes communal witness.

Endurance over outrage does not eliminate urgency. It redefines it. Urgency becomes commitment to long-term formation rather than short-term reaction. It becomes investment in discipleship rather than fixation on headlines.

The erosion of shared truth described earlier in this book unfolded incrementally. It advanced through countless small concessions and quiet redefinitions. Renewal, if it comes, will likely unfold in similar fashion—through countless small acts of courage, integrity, and patience.

National transformation is downstream of personal steadiness. Cultural rebuilding is downstream of character. Institutions reflect the convictions of those who inhabit them.

If believers desire to see healthier civic life, more coherent public discourse, and more stable moral foundations, they must first embody those qualities themselves. Outrage cannot produce what endurance can.

The future will not be shaped primarily by the loudest voices but by the most faithful ones.

This chapter began with a simple question: Will I remain faithful?

That question precedes strategy. It precedes reform plans. It precedes cultural analysis. It is personal before it is public.

Courage in ordinary faithfulness—lived in families, vocations, and speech, sustained through endurance rather than outrage—forms the groundwork upon which any meaningful cultural renewal must stand.

The Cost of Conviction

Courage becomes visible when conviction carries cost.

In recent years, several high-profile legal cases have highlighted the tension between conscience and public expectation. While these cases differ in context and complexity, they illustrate that questions of truth and conviction are no longer confined to private belief.

In Masterpiece Cakeshop v. Colorado Civil Rights Commission (2018), a Colorado baker declined to create a custom wedding cake for a same-sex ceremony, citing religious conviction. The case reached the United States Supreme Court, which ruled that the state commission had shown hostility toward his religious beliefs in its handling of the case. The Court's decision did not resolve every future dispute about similar conflicts, but it affirmed that religious neutrality must be maintained in adjudicating such matters.

Similarly, in 303 Creative LLC v. Elenis (2023), the Supreme Court addressed whether a website designer could be compelled to create custom expressive content that conflicted with her religious convictions. The Court ruled that the First Amendment protects against compelled speech in such contexts. Again, the decision was specific, but it demonstrated how conscience claims increasingly intersect with public commerce.

These cases are often framed politically, yet at their core they involve individuals navigating conviction within professional life. Regardless of how one evaluates each ruling, they illustrate that the cost of standing firm can include legal scrutiny, financial burden, and prolonged public attention.

Other situations unfold without Supreme Court involvement. In 2022, the Supreme Court ruled in Kennedy v. Bremerton School District that a public high school football coach's post-game prayer on the field was protected under the First Amendment. The case involved questions about public expression of faith within government employment. While the legal details were complex, the broader reality was clear: personal religious expression in public roles is increasingly contested.

Beyond legal cases, countless situations occur quietly. Educators navigating pronoun policies. Healthcare professionals wrestling with ethical directives. Employees asked to affirm statements inconsistent with their beliefs. In many instances, resolution occurs through internal negotiation rather than litigation. The cost may not be public but remains real—strained relationships, career limitation, reputational tension.

Acknowledging these realities does not require dramatization. Most believers will not face national headlines. Yet many will encounter moments where silence would preserve comfort and speech would risk misunderstanding.

The presence of cost clarifies the meaning of courage. If conviction carries no consequence, it requires little endurance. When consequence emerges—even modestly—the temptation to soften clarity grows stronger.

Scripture does not romanticize cost, nor does it minimize it. Jesus warned His followers that allegiance to Him could produce division, even within households (Matthew 10:34–36). The warning was not an invitation to hostility but a sober recognition that truth creates differentiation.

At the same time, Scripture anchors believers in hope rather than fear. "Blessed are those who are persecuted for righteousness' sake,"

Jesus said, "for theirs is the kingdom of heaven" (Matthew 5:10). The promise shifts perspective from immediate consequence to ultimate allegiance.

For modern believers, the cost may be subtle rather than severe. A reputation labeled "outdated." A promotion bypassed. A social circle narrowed. These experiences are not equivalent to historic persecution. They are, however, formative.

The question is not whether cost exists. It does. The question is whether believers are prepared for it.

Preparation begins with clarity. Convictions examined deeply are less likely to collapse under pressure. Communities that support one another reduce isolation. Leaders who acknowledge cost honestly prevent surprise and disillusionment.

Cost also refines tone. When believers recognize that faithfulness may require sacrifice, triumphalism fades. Posturing becomes unnecessary. Steadiness replaces aggression.

Courage grounded in realism differs from reaction fueled by grievance. It accepts that tension is part of cultural transition. It refuses both panic and surrender.

Clarity of Conscience

Conviction without clarity can produce confusion. Not every disagreement requires the same response. Wisdom discerns when to speak publicly, when to seek private dialogue, and when to step away.

Conscience is not merely personal preference. It is the internal faculty that evaluates alignment with perceived moral truth. For believers, conscience must be shaped by Scripture rather than by impulse. Romans 12:2 urges transformation through renewal of the mind. A renewed mind strengthens conscience.

Clarity of conscience involves preparation before conflict arises. Waiting until pressure mounts to determine conviction often leads to reactive decisions. Disciplined reflection beforehand provides stability when tension surfaces.

This clarity also guards against unnecessary escalation. Some cultural disagreements require firm public dissent. Others allow for quiet coexistence. Discernment distinguishes between core theological commitments and secondary preferences.

Leaders especially must cultivate such discernment. Congregations watch how pastors and public voices navigate controversy. Overreaction can erode credibility. Silence in essential matters can erode trust. Balance is not weakness; it is maturity.

Ultimately, clarity of conscience and endurance under cost converge. Together they form the backbone of ordinary courage.

The Decision Before Us

Every generation faces defining pressures. Rarely do those pressures announce themselves with clarity. They arrive gradually—through normalized language, shifting expectations, and quiet accommodation. The cumulative effect becomes visible only in retrospect.

This generation's defining pressure concerns truth itself.

Will believers treat truth as negotiable when inconvenient? Will they redefine conviction to preserve comfort? Or will they remain steady when cultural momentum runs in another direction?

The decision is rarely dramatic. It unfolds in ordinary settings. It appears in conversations not broadcast online. It surfaces in meetings where language could be softened to avoid tension. It emerges in classrooms where silence would cost nothing and clarity might cost something.

The future described in earlier chapters—national coherence weakened or strengthened—depends not only on policy or leadership but on these individual moments.

Courage in ordinary faithfulness is cumulative. One decision to speak carefully. One refusal to compromise integrity. One act of patient endurance. Multiplied across communities, these decisions form cultural undercurrents more powerful than episodic outrage.

History demonstrates that societies rarely collapse from a single event. They drift through countless incremental choices. Renewal, if it comes, follows the same pattern. It is built through steady conviction rather than emotional surges.

The question, therefore, is not whether cultural tension will continue. It will. The question is whether believers will anchor themselves deeply enough to withstand it without losing love.

This anchoring requires spiritual discipline. It requires remembering that identity is received, not invented. It requires trusting that truth is grounded in a God who does not change. It requires believing that obedience is not futility, even when immediate results are invisible.

For pastors and leaders, the responsibility is intensified. Congregations look for tone as much as content. If leaders panic, communities fracture. If leaders harden, communities polarize. If leaders model steadiness, communities learn endurance.

For parents, the responsibility is formative. Children absorb whether conviction is lived calmly or defensively. They observe whether disagreement produces fear or thoughtful engagement. Long before they articulate doctrine, they internalize posture.

For professionals, the responsibility is vocational. Integrity at work, consistency in speech, and refusal to caricature opponents contribute quietly to public trust. Cultural rebuilding begins in boardrooms and classrooms long before it reaches legislatures.

The path forward will not be glamorous. It will not trend. It will not generate constant affirmation. But it will generate stability.

Endurance over outrage.

Clarity over ambiguity.

Conviction without hostility.

Love without compromise.

These qualities rarely dominate headlines. Yet they shape generations.

Cultural change begins with personal decision. National renewal begins with individual steadiness. Institutional rebuilding begins with character.

The question remains simple, though its implications are vast:

Will we remain faithful?

The next chapter turns from personal courage to collective rebuilding —what happens when communities shaped by such steadiness begin to influence the institutions around them.

7

REBUILDING WHAT DRIFT HAS WEAKENED

Cultural change does not occur in isolation. It is mediated through institutions. Schools, churches, media organizations, corporations, civic bodies, and families all function as transmitters of moral imagination. They do not merely reflect society; they shape it.

When shared assumptions about truth begin to erode, institutions often adjust before individuals fully recognize the shift. Policies change. Language evolves. Curricula are revised. Narratives are reframed. Over time, these adjustments recalibrate what feels normal.

If renewal is to move beyond personal conviction, it must address institutional formation.

Institutions are powerful precisely because they operate quietly. A classroom does not simply convey information; it conveys worldview. A newsroom does not merely report events; it frames interpretation. A church does not only host gatherings; it shapes conscience. A corporation does not simply produce goods; it establishes internal norms about speech and belief.

When institutions drift from stable conceptions of truth, the effects multiply.

This is not new. Throughout history, educational systems, religious establishments, and media networks have played central roles in shaping public life. In every era, whoever influences formation influences the future.

Rebuilding what drift has weakened therefore requires patient engagement with the structures that transmit culture.

Institutions Shape Imagination

Before policies shift dramatically, imagination shifts subtly. What people believe to be possible, normal, or inevitable often changes long before laws codify those beliefs.

Institutions cultivate that imagination.

Consider education. Public education in the United States has evolved significantly over the past century, influenced by philosophical movements ranging from classical liberalism to progressive educational theory. Curriculum decisions—whether in literature, history, civics, or social development—inevitably reflect judgments about human nature and moral responsibility. These judgments shape students' understanding of authority, freedom, and identity.

This is not inherently sinister. Every educational system reflects a worldview. The question is not whether worldview exists, but which worldview guides formation.

Similarly, churches shape imagination through preaching, discipleship, and communal practice. If teaching grows vague on foundational questions—human nature, sin, redemption, moral order—congregational clarity weakens. Drift within churches often precedes drift in surrounding culture, because churches are meant to anchor moral reasoning.

Corporate and professional institutions also influence imagination. Internal training programs, diversity frameworks, and communication policies shape assumptions about language and identity. These structures can either encourage open, respectful disagreement or subtly discourage dissent. The tone set at institutional levels filters downward.

Rebuilding institutions, then, is not primarily about reclaiming dominance. It is about restoring coherence.

Coherence means that policies align with clearly articulated principles. It means that leaders understand the worldview implications of institutional decisions. It means that moral vocabulary is defined rather than assumed.

Institutional rebuilding begins with leaders willing to think structurally rather than reactively.

Education and Formation

Education remains one of the most formative institutions in any society. What children and young adults are taught—explicitly and implicitly—shapes generational direction.

Debates over curriculum are often framed as political, yet they are fundamentally philosophical. What is the purpose of education? Is it primarily skill acquisition? Civic preparation? Moral formation? Personal self-expression? The answer to that question determines content and method.

In recent decades, conversations around identity, autonomy, and self-definition have become more prominent in educational settings. Policies concerning student privacy, parental involvement, and language use have generated public debate in various states and districts. While implementation differs widely across regions, the broader pattern illustrates that educational institutions increasingly serve as arenas where foundational moral questions are contested.

Rebuilding educational coherence does not require hostility toward educators. Many teachers operate within complex systems and seek to serve students faithfully. It does require clarity about first principles.

If education divorces freedom from responsibility, autonomy from accountability, or identity from biological and moral realities, confusion follows. If education reconnects knowledge with virtue, learning with character, it strengthens civic life.

Parents, pastors, and community leaders must therefore engage education thoughtfully. Engagement can take multiple forms: involvement in local school boards, development of alternative schooling models, support for educators committed to intellectual honesty, and cultivation of strong home-based formation.

The goal is not withdrawal from public life but participation with clarity.

Educational reform, like all institutional reform, unfolds slowly. It requires patience, dialogue, and principled leadership. It also requires courage, particularly when institutional momentum resists examination.

The Church as Moral Anchor

If educational institutions shape intellectual formation, the church shapes moral and spiritual formation. Its influence may be less centralized than in previous eras, but its responsibility remains unchanged.

When cultural assumptions shift, the church faces a dual temptation. One temptation is accommodation—softening doctrine to reduce tension. The other is isolation—retreating into internal language disconnected from public life. Both responses weaken long-term credibility.

The church functions most effectively as a moral anchor when it maintains theological clarity while engaging culture thoughtfully. Clarity does not require volume. It requires coherence.

A church that teaches consistently about human dignity, created order, sin, redemption, and moral responsibility provides its members with a framework capable of navigating contested issues. Without that framework, believers are left to improvise responses based on emotion or political alignment.

Institutional rebuilding begins inside congregations.

Preaching that avoids difficult passages may temporarily reduce discomfort, but it produces long-term fragility. Likewise, preaching that fixates on cultural controversy without grounding in the broader narrative of Scripture risks distortion. The task is balance: teaching the whole counsel of God in a way that forms conscience.

Discipleship structures matter as well. Churches that cultivate deep community—through small groups, mentoring, and intergenerational engagement—build resilience. When believers are known, challenged, and supported, they are less likely to be destabilized by cultural volatility.

The church's credibility also depends on integrity. Public moral critique rings hollow if internal accountability is weak. Institutional health requires transparency, humility, and consistent ethical standards. Scandals within religious leadership have, in recent decades, eroded public trust. Rebuilding influence therefore begins with rebuilding integrity.

A morally coherent church does not dominate culture. It stabilizes it.

Media and the Battle for Narrative

Few institutions shape modern imagination more powerfully than media. The term "media" encompasses traditional journalism, digital platforms, entertainment industries, and social networks. Together, these ecosystems influence what people see, how events are framed, and which narratives gain prominence.

Media does not merely report reality; it interprets it. Editorial choices—what stories to highlight, which voices to amplify, how headlines are worded—shape perception. This dynamic is not inherently malicious. Interpretation is unavoidable. The concern arises when speed, competition, and ideological framing distort complexity.

Contemporary media operates within economic incentives that reward engagement. Digital platforms monetize attention. Stories that provoke strong emotional response—particularly outrage or fear—tend to spread more rapidly. Nuance, which requires patience, struggles to compete in such an environment.

The result is often polarization. Issues become simplified into binary conflict. Opposing perspectives are reduced to caricature. Moral disagreement is framed as moral failure. Over time, trust in media institutions declines, as documented in surveys by organizations such as Gallup and Pew Research Center. Across political lines, Americans report lower confidence in news organizations than in previous decades.

When trust erodes, suspicion increases. When suspicion increases, shared narrative fragments.

Rebuilding what drift has weakened therefore includes media literacy and media integrity.

For individuals, this means cultivating discernment. Not every headline reflects full context. Responsible engagement requires seeking multiple sources, resisting reflexive sharing, and distinguishing between reporting and commentary.

For Christian leaders and institutions, it also means participating constructively in public discourse. Withdrawal cedes narrative entirely to others. Yet participation must avoid mimicking the very incentives that distort truth. Calm, accurate communication—though less sensational—builds long-term credibility.

There is also opportunity. Digital platforms allow voices outside traditional gatekeeping structures to contribute to public conversation. Thoughtful writers, educators, and leaders can shape narrative responsibly. The challenge is resisting the pressure to trade depth for attention.

Media ecosystems will not be transformed overnight. Yet institutions and individuals can model alternative approaches: accuracy over exaggeration, dialogue over derision, clarity over clickbait.

Civic Integrity and Leadership

Institutions do not sustain themselves without leadership. Civic integrity depends on individuals willing to serve with principle rather than expediency.

Leadership in a polarized age requires unusual steadiness. Public officials, nonprofit directors, business executives, and community organizers operate within environments of constant scrutiny. Decisions are often interpreted through partisan lenses, regardless of intent. The temptation is to govern by reaction—responding primarily to pressure rather than principle.

Rebuilding institutional health requires leaders who think long-term. It requires commitment to procedural fairness, transparency, and respect for dissent. When institutions treat disagreement as disloyalty, they weaken internal trust.

Christian engagement in civic life must therefore be marked by integrity. Participation in public service is not inherently partisan. It is a form of stewardship. The aim is not to sacralize political power but to exercise responsibility faithfully within existing structures.

Civic institutions flourish when citizens believe processes are fair, voices are heard, and truth is not manipulated for short-term gain. When trust deteriorates, stability erodes.

Rebuilding civic integrity will involve difficult conversations about authority, accountability, and restraint. It will require leaders who refuse to inflame division for advantage and who resist the reduction of every moral question to partisan allegiance.

Institutional reform is complex. It unfolds gradually. Yet the direction of that reform depends on whether leaders value coherence over convenience.

Generational Investment and Leadership Formation

Institutions rarely decline because of a single policy decision. They decline because formation weakens across generations. The rebuilding of institutional health therefore begins with leadership formation.

Every institution—school, church, newsroom, corporation, civic body—reflects the worldview of those who lead it. If leaders lack moral clarity, institutions drift. If leaders lack intellectual depth, institutions simplify complex issues into slogans. If leaders lack integrity, institutions lose trust.

Rebuilding what drift has weakened requires long-term investment in people, not simply structural reform.

Churches must think beyond weekly programming and consider leadership pipelines. Who is being discipled not only for personal faith but for public responsibility? Are young believers encouraged to pursue vocations in education, law, journalism, medicine, public service, and academia with theological grounding? Or is public life treated as peripheral to spiritual calling?

Historically, moments of cultural renewal were accompanied by serious intellectual engagement. Universities once emerged from religious conviction about the coherence of truth. The fragmentation of disciplines over time has contributed to the separation of moral reasoning from public discourse. Rebuilding intellectual credibility will require Christians who are both academically competent and theologically anchored.

This does not mean retreating into parallel systems exclusively. It means equipping believers to enter existing institutions with clarity. Influence is not gained through complaint alone. It grows through competence combined with conviction.

Mentorship is central to this process. Younger leaders benefit from older voices who have navigated tension without surrendering integrity. Intergenerational transfer prevents cycles of reinvention. It also guards against reactionary swings. Experience tempers zeal; zeal prevents stagnation.

The long view reshapes expectation. Institutional rebuilding may take decades. The goal is not immediate dominance but durable presence. Cultural imagination is shaped gradually through repetition of faithful practice.

Media Literacy and Narrative Responsibility

If media ecosystems shape public perception, then responsible engagement requires literacy. Media literacy does not mean suspicion of every outlet. It means awareness of framing, incentive structures, and narrative construction.

Digital platforms prioritize engagement. Content that provokes strong emotion—particularly anger or fear—spreads quickly. This dynamic affects not only secular media but Christian media as well. When outrage becomes a marketing tool, truth becomes secondary to reaction.

Rebuilding narrative integrity requires restraint.

For pastors and leaders, this begins with modeling careful sourcing. Sharing information without verification undermines credibility. Exaggeration may energize temporarily, but it erodes trust long-term. Responsible communication strengthens witness.

It also involves cultivating congregational discernment. Teaching believers how to evaluate sources, distinguish reporting from commentary, and resist algorithm-driven polarization contributes to institutional health. A congregation that consumes media uncritically becomes reactive. A congregation trained in discernment becomes stable.

There is also opportunity. New platforms allow thoughtful voices to contribute meaningfully without relying solely on legacy structures. Writers, educators, and leaders who communicate with clarity and charity can influence narrative responsibly. Depth may not trend as quickly as outrage, but it sustains influence longer.

Institutional rebuilding in the media sphere therefore requires two commitments: integrity in participation and discernment in consumption.

Rebuilding with Humility and Resolve

Institutional reform can easily drift toward triumphalism. When discussing rebuilding education, media, or civic life, it is tempting to frame the effort as reclamation of control. Such framing undermines credibility and misrepresents Christian calling.

The goal is not dominance. It is coherence.

Coherence means that institutions align practice with clearly articulated moral foundations. It means leaders acknowledge limits of authority. It means dissent is handled respectfully. It means truth is pursued even when politically inconvenient.

Humility strengthens this work. No institution, religious or secular, is immune to error. A commitment to reform must include willingness to correct internal failures. Without humility, rebuilding becomes rebranding.

Resolve is equally necessary. Cultural headwinds will not disappear quickly. Institutional inertia resists change. Patience must accompany persistence.

When communities shaped by personal courage (Chapter 6) begin to serve within institutions with integrity, rebuilding becomes plausible. Families that value truth produce leaders who carry that value into schools and professions. Churches that cultivate depth produce thinkers who contribute to public discourse. Professionals who refuse reactive outrage model alternative leadership.

Institutional health reflects personal character at scale.

Higher Education and the Battle for Ideas

Institutions of higher education occupy a unique role in shaping long-term cultural direction. Universities do not merely grant degrees; they cultivate intellectual frameworks that influence law, journalism, medicine, public policy, and education itself. Ideas incubated within academic settings often filter outward into broader society over time.

Historically, many Western universities emerged from religious foundations. Institutions such as Harvard, Yale, and Princeton were originally established with explicit theological commitments. Over centuries, those commitments evolved, diversified, and in many cases receded from central influence. This historical shift illustrates how institutional identity can transform gradually across generations.

The modern university environment reflects a wide range of philosophical perspectives. Within many disciplines, assumptions about human nature, authority, and moral autonomy shape academic discourse. These assumptions do not remain confined to lecture halls. They influence professional training and public leadership.

Rebuilding intellectual coherence does not require hostility toward academia. It requires participation. Christian scholars, researchers, and students who combine academic excellence with moral clarity contribute to institutional stability. Withdrawal leaves intellectual formation exclusively in the hands of prevailing philosophical trends.

Intellectual depth is essential. Cultural influence without intellectual credibility collapses under scrutiny. Leaders who can articulate why truth is grounded in objective reality—rather than merely asserting that it is—strengthen institutional resilience.

Churches, therefore, should not treat higher education as adversarial territory alone. They should view it as a mission field for thoughtful engagement. Supporting young believers pursuing advanced study, encouraging rigorous scholarship, and fostering dialogue across disciplines contribute to long-term institutional health.

The battle for ideas is rarely resolved quickly. It unfolds through research, publication, mentorship, and patient argument. Yet ideas shape laws and policies long before most citizens recognize their origin. Institutional rebuilding must therefore include intellectual investment.

Technology, Algorithms, and the Attention Economy

No modern institution has shaped moral imagination more rapidly than digital technology. Social media platforms, streaming services, and algorithm-driven content feeds influence not only what individuals consume but how they think.

Unlike traditional media, digital platforms operate through algorithmic curation. Content is not simply presented chronologically; it is prioritized based on engagement metrics. The more a post provokes interaction—clicks, comments, shares—the more widely it spreads. Emotional intensity becomes an advantage.

This structure forms what many analysts describe as the "attention economy." In this system, attention functions as currency. Platforms monetize engagement. Content that holds attention longer or generates stronger reaction yields greater revenue. As a result, material that is provocative, polarizing, or emotionally charged is often amplified.

This incentive structure shapes public discourse in subtle but powerful ways.

Nuance struggles to compete with outrage.

Complexity loses to simplicity.

Measured argument is overshadowed by viral soundbite.

Over time, users adapt to this environment. Attention spans shorten. Patience for extended reasoning diminishes. Identity becomes performative—expressed publicly for validation rather than explored privately for coherence.

The moral implications are significant.

When public conversation is shaped primarily by algorithms optimized for engagement, truth can become secondary to traction. Assertions that confirm prior beliefs spread quickly. Corrective information that complicates narrative spreads more slowly. Polarization intensifies not merely because people disagree, but because technological systems reward emotional escalation.

This does not imply coordinated manipulation by every media actor. It reflects structural incentives. Platforms are engineered to maximize usage. The byproduct is amplification of extremes.

Rebuilding what drift has weakened therefore requires intentional resistance to these incentives.

For individuals, this means cultivating digital discipline. Limiting reactive engagement. Verifying information before sharing. Choosing long-form reading over headline scanning. Refusing to equate visibility with validity.

For churches and leaders, it means modeling alternative communication rhythms. Teaching congregations how digital environments shape perception. Encouraging reflection before reaction. Avoiding the temptation to mirror algorithm-driven outrage in order to grow influence.

There is opportunity within digital technology as well. Thoughtful voices can reach audiences once inaccessible. Educational resources can be distributed widely. Communities can form across geographic distance. The challenge lies not in rejecting technology but in refusing to be shaped uncritically by its incentives.

Institutional rebuilding in the digital age must account for algorithmic formation. If imagination is shaped by attention, then attention must be stewarded intentionally. Without such stewardship, moral reasoning becomes fragmented and reactive.

The health of public discourse depends not only on what is said but on the environment in which it is amplified.

The Formation of Public Conscience

Cultural stability depends not only on institutions, but on the shared moral language that undergirds them. Laws, policies, and organizational structures operate within an invisible framework of assumptions about right and wrong, dignity and harm, freedom and restraint. When that shared moral grammar weakens, institutions struggle to function coherently.

Public conscience is not formed in a single location. It develops through families, religious communities, schools, media narratives, legal reasoning, and cultural storytelling. Over time, these influences create a set of widely recognized moral intuitions. Even those who disagree politically often rely on common language about fairness, justice, responsibility, and human worth.

When shared moral language erodes, disagreement intensifies.

This erosion rarely begins with hostility. It begins with redefinition. Words that once carried relatively stable meanings begin to shift. Freedom becomes autonomy without reference to design. Justice becomes affirmation of preference rather than alignment with principle. Harm becomes subjective discomfort rather than measurable injury. Dignity becomes self-assertion rather than inherent worth.

As definitions fragment, conversation becomes more difficult. Participants in public debate may use identical words while operating from different conceptual frameworks. The result is not merely disagreement over conclusions, but confusion over premises.

Rebuilding culture, therefore, requires more than defending individual positions. It requires restoring shared moral grammar.

This does not mean demanding uniform theological belief in a pluralistic society. It means articulating moral reasoning in ways that appeal to both revelation and natural order. Historically, societies have sustained public discourse by grounding rights and responsibilities in realities understood to be objective, even if interpreted differently across traditions.

When moral claims are severed entirely from any concept of objective order, they become assertions of will. Assertions of will compete. Competition intensifies. Trust declines.

Public conscience weakens when moral reasoning is replaced by emotive signaling. Social media accelerates this pattern. Complex moral debates are compressed into slogans. Nuance is interpreted as compromise. Outrage substitutes for persuasion. Over time, emotional intensity crowds out disciplined argument.

The rebuilding of public conscience requires patience in language.

Leaders must resist rhetorical escalation even when escalation appears effective. Careful speech slows polarization. It clarifies premises. It invites engagement rather than retaliation. When communities model disciplined moral reasoning, they contribute to the stabilization of discourse.

This discipline extends beyond tone. It involves intellectual honesty. When evidence complicates a preferred narrative, integrity demands acknowledgment. When opponents raise legitimate concerns, fairness demands recognition. Such practices do not weaken conviction. They strengthen credibility.

Historically, societies that sustained stable moral frameworks did so by transmitting coherent narratives about human nature. Those narratives explained why dignity mattered, why obligations existed, and why limits were necessary. Without narrative coherence, moral rules appear arbitrary.

The Christian narrative offers such coherence. Creation affirms inherent dignity. The fall explains distortion. Redemption introduces restoration. This framework situates moral teaching within a larger story rather than presenting it as isolated restriction. When articulated carefully in public discourse, it contributes to shared understanding even among those who do not fully affirm its theological claims.

Rebuilding public conscience also requires recovering the concept of virtue. Modern discourse often emphasizes rights without equal emphasis on character. Yet rights depend on responsible exercise. A society that prizes autonomy but neglects virtue risks instability. Virtue forms the habits that allow freedom to flourish.

Educational institutions once prioritized character formation alongside intellectual development. While models have shifted over time, the underlying need remains. Citizens capable of self-governance must cultivate self-discipline. Leaders entrusted with authority must demonstrate restraint. Without virtue, structures falter.

Public conscience is shaped by repetition. Practices repeated across generations become norms. When communities consistently demonstrate fairness, accountability, and respect for truth, those practices gradually influence expectation. Expectations shape institutions. Institutions shape culture.

This process is cumulative.

It rarely produces immediate headlines. It rarely generates viral attention. But over decades, disciplined moral formation recalibrates public expectation.

The task before this generation is therefore not merely to win arguments. It is to model coherence long enough for coherence to regain credibility.

In an environment where moral language is frequently weaponized, steady articulation of principled reasoning becomes countercultural. Yet it is precisely this steadiness that stabilizes.

Rebuilding public conscience will not eliminate disagreement. It will not produce uniformity. It will, however, restore the possibility of reasoned debate grounded in shared recognition that truth exists beyond preference.

Such restoration begins in smaller communities before it shapes broader society. Families teach language. Churches teach narrative. Schools teach reasoning. Media platforms amplify example. Civic leaders reinforce standards. Together, these influences either fragment or stabilize public conscience.

The question is not whether moral language will shape culture. It always does.

The question is whether that language will remain anchored in objective reality — or drift with shifting sentiment.

Rebuilders answer that question not primarily with slogans, but with sustained integrity.

. . .

A Historical Reminder: Institutions Can Be Renewed

Institutional drift is not irreversible. History offers examples of reform that began not with sudden revolution but with sustained moral clarity.

In the nineteenth century, various social reform movements emerged from religious conviction, including abolition efforts in Britain and the United States. While these movements were complex and involved political negotiation, they were fueled by moral argument grounded in theological belief about human dignity. Leaders such as William Wilberforce in Britain operated within existing institutions rather than outside them. Reform unfolded gradually, through legislative persistence and sustained public persuasion.

Similarly, the civil rights movement in the United States drew heavily upon Christian moral language. Churches served as organizing centers, and biblical appeals to justice shaped public discourse. Institutional change followed moral conviction articulated persistently over time.

These historical moments were not flawless. They unfolded amid opposition, compromise, and difficulty. Yet they illustrate an important principle: institutions respond to sustained moral reasoning when leaders combine conviction with endurance.

Renewal did not emerge through outrage alone. It required discipline, organization, and credibility. It required individuals willing to work within structures patiently.

This pattern remains instructive. Institutional rebuilding in the present era will not be instantaneous. It will require leaders willing to think generationally rather than episodically.

Generational Coherence and the Long View

. . .

Institutional health ultimately depends on generational continuity. When moral language shifts every decade, stability erodes. When foundational principles are transmitted clearly across generations, coherence strengthens.

The long view reframes urgency. Instead of asking how to win the next cultural argument, leaders ask how to shape the next twenty years. Instead of reacting to each policy dispute, they invest in education, mentorship, scholarship, and character formation.

Families who teach children disciplined thinking contribute to institutional resilience. Churches that prioritize theological depth contribute to civic stability. Professionals who cultivate intellectual seriousness contribute to public trust.

Generational investment also tempers despair. Cultural volatility can create the impression of rapid collapse. Yet long-term patterns often reveal cycles of challenge and renewal. Patience, informed by history, guards against fatalism.

The rebuilding of institutions requires communities committed to slow growth rather than immediate control. It requires leaders who understand that credibility accumulates gradually.

Media ecosystems may amplify extremes, but institutions rooted in coherence provide counterweight. Educational systems may debate philosophy, but teachers grounded in principle shape classrooms. Civic bodies may fluctuate politically, but leaders committed to integrity stabilize process.

Rebuilding what drift has weakened therefore depends less on spectacle and more on formation.

From Personal Courage to Public Stability

Chapter 6 argued that renewal begins with individual courage. This chapter extends that argument: institutions reflect the character of the people who inhabit them.

When individuals remain steady, institutions stabilize.

When leaders cultivate clarity, policies align with principle.

When communities resist algorithm-driven outrage, public discourse regains texture.

The relationship is reciprocal. Healthy institutions reinforce personal formation. Fragmented institutions accelerate confusion.

The task before this generation is not domination but reconstruction—patient, principled, humble reconstruction. The goal is not uniformity of belief across society but restoration of shared moral grammar sufficient to sustain civic trust.

This reconstruction will not eliminate disagreement. A pluralistic society will always contain moral diversity. The question is whether that diversity operates within a framework that acknowledges objective reality and human dignity, or within one that reduces truth to preference.

Institutional rebuilding therefore demands both conviction and restraint. Conviction provides direction. Restraint preserves credibility.

Institutional Integrity as Cultural Witness

Institutions communicate values not only through mission statements but through behavior. Policies, hiring decisions, internal accountability, transparency practices, and communication tone all convey moral assumptions.

When institutions operate inconsistently—articulating principles publicly while compromising them privately—trust deteriorates.

Cynicism grows not merely because people disagree but because they perceive incoherence.

Rebuilding what drift has weakened therefore requires visible integrity.

For churches, this means financial transparency, moral accountability in leadership, and clear articulation of doctrine without ambiguity. Institutional credibility begins internally.

For educational bodies, it means fostering genuine intellectual inquiry rather than ideological conformity. Classrooms that encourage respectful dissent strengthen long-term stability. Suppression of disagreement weakens it.

For media organizations, it means distinguishing clearly between reporting and commentary, acknowledging error when it occurs, and resisting sensational framing when nuance is required. Accuracy builds trust more slowly than outrage, but it builds it more durably.

For civic institutions, integrity means procedural fairness. When citizens believe rules apply consistently across perspectives, legitimacy strengthens. When processes appear manipulated for advantage, social cohesion erodes.

Institutional integrity is not merely functional; it is formative. It teaches communities what is normal.

If dishonesty becomes routine, dishonesty multiplies.

If humility becomes visible, humility spreads.

If accountability is practiced, responsibility grows.

This is why institutional rebuilding cannot be reduced to political victory. It concerns habits, structures, and standards. It concerns long-term trust.

Trust is fragile. It accumulates slowly and evaporates quickly. Rebuilding it requires patience.

The health of a nation depends less on temporary alignment of power and more on sustained confidence in the institutions that mediate public life. When families trust schools, when citizens trust processes, when congregations trust leadership, stability increases.

Such trust does not demand unanimity. It requires coherence.

Coherence emerges when institutions align their practices with clearly articulated moral foundations. It is weakened when expediency overrides principle.

The rebuilding envisioned in this chapter is therefore moral before it is political. It begins with leaders who value consistency over convenience and with communities willing to hold institutions accountable respectfully.

8

ENDURING TRUTH
IN A RESTLESS AGE

The question before us is not whether cultural turbulence exists. It does. The more important question is whether turbulence defines the future.

History rarely moves in straight lines. Periods of moral clarity are often followed by seasons of confusion. Institutions strengthen and weaken. Ideas rise and fall. Yet beneath these fluctuations, deeper currents endure. Truth does not evaporate because it is contested. Reality does not dissolve because it is reinterpreted.

The present moment feels unstable because shared assumptions have fractured. As earlier chapters have shown, the relocation of authority—from revelation to internal perception—has reshaped identity, morality, and institutional life. The result is fragmentation. But fragmentation is not final.

Every generation inherits both strengths and weaknesses. We did not invent expressive individualism. We inherited it. We did not initiate every institutional drift. We stepped into it. The responsibility of this generation is not to lament endlessly but to rebuild wisely.

Rebuilding begins with clarity.

If truth is revealed and grounded in the character of God, then it remains steady even when culture shifts. It does not require reinvention. It requires reaffirmation. The work ahead is not creative in the sense of designing a new moral order. It is restorative in the sense of returning to what has always been true.

This restoration will not occur through outrage. Outrage can draw attention, but it rarely produces endurance. Nor will it occur through withdrawal. Retreat leaves institutions to be shaped by whatever voices remain. The path forward is steadier: faithful presence.

Faithful presence means inhabiting existing institutions with conviction and composure. It means fathers teaching children patiently. It means pastors preaching Scripture without apology and without hostility. It means educators approaching their vocation with intellectual seriousness and moral courage. It means professionals acting with integrity even when incentives reward compromise.

The temptation in restless ages is to mirror the restlessness. To respond to volatility with volatility. To answer escalation with escalation. Yet the most transformative voices in history were rarely frantic. They were steady.

Consider the early church. It emerged within a pluralistic and often hostile empire. Christians did not possess political dominance. They did not control media platforms. They did not command cultural prestige. What they possessed was coherence—belief rooted in revelation, embodied in community, sustained through suffering. Their stability outlasted the instability of their environment.

The same principle applies today. A community anchored in objective truth becomes a stabilizing force within a shifting culture. Not because it is loud, but because it is consistent.

Consistency builds trust. Trust builds influence. Influence, over time, shapes institutions.

This shaping is rarely dramatic. It is incremental. It occurs when families model fidelity across decades. It occurs when churches resist the pressure to dilute doctrine for short-term comfort. It occurs when leaders prioritize long-term integrity over immediate approval.

The rebuilding envisioned here is generational.

We are unlikely to see complete cultural realignment in a single news cycle or election season. But generational formation can recalibrate direction. Children raised within coherent moral frameworks carry those frameworks into adulthood. Congregations grounded in Scripture raise leaders who shape schools, businesses, and civic life.

The alternative—reactive resistance without constructive formation—produces fatigue. Constant alarm exhausts communities. Sustainable rebuilding requires rhythm: teaching, mentoring, serving, praying, persevering.

In practical terms, this means strengthening the ordinary structures that sustain truth.

Families must reclaim intentional formation. Conversations about identity, dignity, and morality cannot be outsourced entirely to schools or screens. Parents who understand the philosophical shifts shaping culture can equip their children not merely to react, but to reason.

Churches must deepen theological literacy. Surface-level familiarity with Scripture will not withstand sustained cultural pressure. Believers need to understand not only what they believe, but why. They need to see how doctrines connect—creation, fall, redemption, restoration—so that moral teaching flows from a coherent narrative rather than isolated rules.

Educational institutions that affirm classical learning and intellectual humility can contribute significantly to rebuilding. Teaching students how to think, not merely what to think, cultivates resilience. Exposure to competing ideas, examined carefully and honestly, strengthens conviction rather than weakens it.

Media literacy is also essential. The attention economy rewards immediacy and outrage. Rebuilders must cultivate discipline—

slower reading, thoughtful engagement, refusal to amplify misinformation. Institutions that value accuracy over speed regain credibility over time.

None of these practices will trend quickly. They do not produce instant cultural victory. But they produce stability. And stability, sustained across decades, alters trajectory.

The temptation in any period of rapid change is to believe that the future will simply extend the present. If confusion dominates today, it is easy to assume confusion will dominate tomorrow. History suggests otherwise. Ideas that appear dominant can fade when their internal contradictions become clear. Trends that feel permanent can weaken when their foundations prove unstable.

Truth, by contrast, does not depend on trend.

The Christian claim has always been countercultural in some sense. It affirms that reality is grounded not in human will but in divine authority. That conviction has endured across empires, persecutions, and philosophical revolutions. It has survived because it rests not on popularity but on revelation.

If the church remains anchored in that revelation, it can serve as a stabilizing presence in a restless age.

The task is not to reclaim dominance. It is to cultivate durability.

Durability is built through ordinary faithfulness—through marriages that endure, friendships that reconcile, leaders who repent when wrong, institutions that correct error rather than defend it.

Cultural change often begins quietly. A generation chooses to take truth seriously. Families commit to formation. Churches recommit to doctrine. Schools recommit to intellectual rigor. Over time, these commitments accumulate.

Rebuilding requires patience because it works against the logic of the attention economy. It values long obedience over short bursts of intensity. It privileges depth over speed.

The question for this generation is therefore not whether turbulence exists. It is whether we will respond with equal turbulence or with steadiness.

The chapters behind us have examined the philosophical relocation of truth and its consequences. The chapters ahead must ask what endurance looks like in practice.

If truth is not self-defined but revealed, then it remains available. It remains steady. It remains sufficient.

The work before us is not to invent a new moral order.

It is to live faithfully within the one that already exists.

Rebuilding the Family as the First Institution

Every durable culture rests upon the health of its households. Before policy, before media, before educational systems, the family forms the moral imagination of a child. If truth is to endure, it must first be taught across a kitchen table.

Rebuilding begins with intentional formation. Parents cannot assume cultural neutrality. Children are absorbing messages about identity, authority, and morality long before they articulate them. Screens introduce ideas earlier than schools. Schools reinforce ideas long before adulthood. If families remain passive, formation will occur by default.

Intentional formation does not require paranoia. It requires presence. Conversations about truth, dignity, embodiment, and responsibility must be normal rather than reactive. Children who understand why their family believes what it believes are less likely to experience inherited conviction as arbitrary restriction.

Family stability also models coherence. Marriages marked by forgiveness, discipline practiced with consistency, and moral standards applied with humility teach more than lectures. A home grounded in both truth and love becomes a living argument for objective reality.

Rebuilding culture without rebuilding families is impossible.

Regrounding the Church in Theological Depth

The church cannot stabilize a restless age if it is itself doctrinally uncertain. Clarity does not require harshness, but it does require courage. Sermons that avoid difficult passages for fear of offense may produce temporary comfort, but they do not cultivate resilience.

Theological depth is not academic luxury; it is cultural necessity. Congregations must understand the arc of Scripture, not merely its isolated commands. Creation establishes order. The fall introduces distortion. Redemption restores alignment. Restoration promises renewal. Without that framework, moral teaching can feel arbitrary rather than coherent.

Leaders must also model intellectual humility. The church should not fear questions. It should welcome them, examine them carefully, and answer them patiently. Confidence in revealed truth allows space for inquiry without panic.

Churches that maintain both conviction and compassion become sanctuaries of stability in unstable environments.

Reforming Education Toward Intellectual Honesty

Educational institutions shape future leaders. Whether in public schools, private academies, or homeschools, the task is not indoctrination but formation in disciplined thinking.

Students should learn how ideas develop historically and how philosophical assumptions influence policy. Exposure to competing worldviews, examined critically rather than emotionally, strengthens intellectual maturity. When students understand the roots of expressive individualism, they are better equipped to engage it thoughtfully rather than reactively.

Intellectual honesty requires acknowledging complexity. Cultural debates rarely reduce to caricature. Teaching students to analyze arguments carefully, to distinguish fact from interpretation, and to resist rhetorical exaggeration builds citizens capable of sustaining civil discourse.

Rebuilding requires thinkers, not merely defenders.

Restoring Integrity in Public Leadership

Civic institutions lose credibility when principle yields to expediency. Rebuilding trust demands leaders who value consistency over convenience.

This applies across political and professional spheres. Laws must be interpreted carefully. Policies must be articulated clearly. Disagreement must be addressed without dehumanization. Procedural fairness matters because it signals commitment to shared standards rather than shifting advantage.

Leadership integrity is contagious. When citizens observe humility and accountability in public officials, cynicism weakens. When institutions correct error transparently, trust grows.

The rebuilding envisioned here is not partisan. It is principled.

Resisting the Distortions of the Attention Economy

· · ·

The digital environment amplifies volatility. Algorithms reward emotional intensity and rapid reaction. If rebuilding is to succeed, individuals and institutions must resist being shaped by that incentive structure.

Slower communication can be more responsible communication. Verifying information before sharing it protects credibility. Prioritizing long-form reasoning over viral fragments cultivates depth.

Leaders who refuse to mirror outrage may initially appear quieter, but over time they gain authority. Stability attracts those exhausted by constant escalation.

Rebuilding culture requires disciplined attention.

Cultivating Generational Patience

Perhaps the most difficult aspect of rebuilding is patience. Cultural correction rarely unfolds in a single season. It often requires decades of faithful presence.

Generational patience does not mean passivity. It means endurance. It recognizes that formation outlasts reaction. The children shaped today become the teachers, pastors, and policymakers of tomorrow.

History demonstrates that societies recalibrate gradually. Ideas that dominate one decade may weaken in the next. Institutions that drift can reform under sustained pressure from principled leadership.

The responsibility of this generation is not to secure immediate triumph. It is to secure durable foundations.

How Cultures Recalibrate

. . .

Cultural drift rarely announces itself in dramatic language. It unfolds gradually, often unnoticed until its consequences accumulate. In the same way, cultural recalibration rarely arrives with spectacle. It develops quietly, as assumptions are examined, as contradictions surface, and as committed communities live differently long enough to influence their surroundings.

History shows that enduring change is seldom driven by numerical majorities at the outset. It is shaped by disciplined minorities who remain coherent while broader culture wavers. Ideas do not reshape civilizations overnight. They spread through institutions, through education, through families, and through steady example.

Movements that endure share common characteristics. They are intellectually grounded. They are morally consistent. They are patient. They resist the temptation to mirror the volatility of their opposition. And they cultivate leaders who think beyond the immediate moment.

Consider how major philosophical shifts have occurred in the past. Enlightenment rationalism did not displace medieval assumptions in a single generation. It advanced through universities, pamphlets, salons, and correspondence networks. Industrialization reshaped social structures over decades, not weeks. Civil rights reform required sustained moral argument, organized communities, and long-term legislative engagement.

In each case, recalibration required persistence.

This pattern is instructive. Cultural renewal is not achieved by winning every debate. It is achieved by demonstrating coherence over time. When prevailing frameworks fail to provide stability, people begin to search for alternatives. If an alternative has been cultivated patiently—intellectually serious, morally consistent, relationally embodied—it becomes credible.

Rebuilding, therefore, is not reactionary resistance. It is constructive presence.

Constructive presence means investing in institutions even when outcomes are uncertain. It means training children in disciplined reasoning even when surrounding culture prizes immediacy. It means producing scholarship, art, education, and service rooted in enduring truth rather than trend.

It also requires realism about cost.

Endurance is not comfortable. Faithfulness may invite misunderstanding. Institutional reform often meets resistance. Those who choose coherence over convenience may face marginalization before they experience influence.

Yet influence secured without endurance is fragile.

One of the defining features of the modern attention economy is its acceleration. Trends rise and collapse rapidly. Outrage cycles refresh daily. Algorithms reward immediacy rather than durability. In such an environment, patience appears weak.

It is not weak.

Patience is strategic.

Communities that refuse to be driven by the emotional tempo of digital platforms cultivate stability. Stability attracts those exhausted by volatility. Over time, steadiness builds trust. Trust builds authority. Authority shapes institutions.

Cultural recalibration also requires moral credibility. If communities advocating objective truth fail to practice integrity internally, their external critique collapses. Hypocrisy undermines coherence. Renewal must begin within.

The church, therefore, must examine itself even as it engages culture. Families must practice the stability they advocate publicly. Leaders must embody the humility they call for in others. Rebuilding loses force when rhetoric exceeds character.

Another principle of recalibration is intergenerational continuity.

Ideas persist when they are transmitted intentionally. Every generation interprets inherited convictions through the lens of its own challenges. Without deliberate teaching, assumptions erode. Without explanation, tradition feels arbitrary.

This is why formation matters more than reaction.

Reaction responds to headlines. Formation shapes worldview. Headlines fade; worldview endures.

When families discuss not only what they believe but why, when churches teach doctrine as a coherent narrative rather than isolated rules, when educators cultivate intellectual rigor instead of ideological conformity, a generation emerges capable of sustained leadership.

Such leadership does not seek dominance. It seeks alignment with reality.

History also demonstrates that dominant ideas often weaken when their internal tensions become visible. Philosophical frameworks that promise liberation but produce fragmentation eventually face scrutiny. Systems that elevate autonomy but erode trust encounter instability. When contradictions accumulate, space opens for alternative foundations.

That space is filled by those prepared to inhabit it.

Preparation requires discipline long before opportunity appears.

Rebuilding is therefore an act of faithfulness rather than prediction. It does not assume guaranteed cultural reversal. It assumes responsibility regardless of outcome.

The measure of success is not immediate transformation but durable witness.

In practical terms, this means resisting both despair and overconfidence. Despair withdraws prematurely. Overconfidence overestimates speed. Endurance navigates between them.

Communities anchored in revealed truth need not panic when cultural tides shift. Nor should they presume inevitability of correction. They are called to steady presence—to teach, to serve, to lead, to think, to pray, to persevere.

Over time, such presence reshapes expectation.

What begins as minority conviction can become normative assumption. What appears countercultural in one generation may become foundational in another. The recalibration of culture is rarely dramatic. It is cumulative.

And cumulative change is built by those who refuse to abandon coherence when confusion feels dominant.

Rebuilding, then, is not about reclaiming an idealized past. It is about restoring alignment between human life and enduring truth. It is about ensuring that institutions reflect stable foundations rather than shifting preference.

The question before this generation is not whether turbulence exists. It is whether we will respond with equal turbulence or with disciplined endurance.

Cultural recalibration does not require spectacle.

It requires steadiness sustained long enough to outlast the moment.

The work of rebuilding does not begin with institutions. It begins with individuals who choose steadiness over reaction.

Every era tempts its people to believe that urgency is the same as importance. In restless ages, loud voices are mistaken for strong ones. Yet strength is not measured by volume. It is measured by endurance.

If truth is not self-defined but revealed, then it does not require panic to defend it. It requires faithfulness to embody it.

Rebuilding culture is not a project for the impatient. It is a calling for the disciplined. It asks fathers to remain present when distraction is easier. It asks mothers to shape moral imagination when cultural narratives pull in other directions. It asks pastors to preach difficult passages when silence would draw less criticism. It asks educators to pursue intellectual honesty when ideological conformity promises approval.

This is not dramatic work. It is ordinary work done consistently.

Cultural recalibration begins when enough people choose formation over frenzy.

The temptation in times of fragmentation is to respond with fragmentation of our own—to divide quickly, to assume motives, to treat disagreement as betrayal. Yet rebuilding demands composure. A steady voice carries further than a reactive one.

The Christian claim has always rested on permanence rather than popularity. The gospel did not emerge in a stable moral climate. It emerged in a world marked by competing philosophies and moral confusion. Its endurance was not secured through cultural dominance but through transformed lives and coherent communities.

The same pattern holds today.

If believers live with integrity—if marriages endure, if leaders admit fault when wrong, if churches teach Scripture carefully rather than selectively—credibility grows. It may grow slowly. It may grow quietly. But it grows.

Cultural trust is rebuilt not through viral moments but through visible consistency.

This requires rejecting two extremes.

The first is despair. Despair assumes that drift is irreversible. It imagines that once truth is contested, it cannot regain clarity. History does not support that assumption. Ideas rise and fall. Philosophies dominate and recede. Cultural confidence shifts. Truth outlasts each cycle.

The second extreme is triumphalism. Triumphalism assumes that correction is inevitable and effortless. It confuses conviction with guarantee. Rebuilding requires labor. It requires sacrifice. It requires patience.

Between despair and triumphalism lies responsibility.

Responsibility is quieter. It does not demand instant results. It demands steady obedience.

If you are a parent, responsibility looks like conversation. It looks like teaching your children not only what you believe, but why. It looks like modeling repentance when you fail and humility when corrected.

If you are a pastor, responsibility looks like preaching the full counsel of God—not selectively, not defensively, but faithfully. It looks like forming congregations capable of reasoning rather than merely reacting.

If you are an educator, responsibility looks like cultivating disciplined thinking. It looks like encouraging students to examine claims carefully, to distinguish evidence from assertion, and to resist the simplifications that dominate digital spaces.

If you serve in public life, responsibility looks like integrity. It looks like procedural fairness, careful language, and refusal to dehumanize opponents.

None of these actions will feel revolutionary in isolation. Together, sustained across time, they are transformative.

Cultural change rarely begins with sweeping gestures. It begins with durable commitments.

The rebuilding of shared moral understanding does not require uniform agreement on every policy question. It requires something deeper: a renewed recognition that truth exists beyond preference, that dignity is grounded beyond consensus, and that freedom flourishes best within reality rather than against it.

If enough communities embody that recognition, institutions adjust.

If enough leaders value coherence over convenience, public discourse stabilizes.

If enough families practice intentional formation, generational direction shifts.

This is not naive optimism. It is historical observation. Societies that rediscover their foundations often do so gradually, through disciplined minority influence rather than dramatic majority reversal.

The task before this generation is not to win every argument. It is to preserve what is enduring.

Truth does not need embellishment. It needs fidelity.

Love does not require dilution of conviction. It requires clarity expressed with humility.

Courage is not loud. It is steady.

And rebuilding is not glamorous. It is faithful.

There may never be a headline announcing that cultural confusion has ended. There may never be a moment when everyone agrees that foundations have been restored. But there will be families who live differently. There will be churches that remain clear. There will be institutions that regain trust because individuals within them chose integrity.

That is how cultures recalibrate.

Not through spectacle.

Through steadiness.

The future will not be shaped primarily by those who shout the loudest, but by those who endure the longest.

Truth has endured before.

It will endure again.

CONCLUSION
THE WORK THAT REMAINS

Every generation believes its moment is uniquely fragile.

History suggests otherwise.

Civilizations have always wrestled with authority, identity, and truth. Ideas have always competed. Institutions have always drifted and reformed. What feels unprecedented is often a new expression of an old tension: whether reality is received or constructed, whether truth is discovered or declared.

This book has argued that the fracture beneath our present turbulence is not primarily political. It is epistemological. It concerns where authority resides. When truth is relocated from revelation to internal perception, fragmentation follows. When identity becomes self-defined rather than received, stability weakens. When institutions adopt competing foundations, coherence erodes.

Yet fragmentation is not destiny.

Truth does not dissolve when it is questioned. It does not weaken because it is contested. It remains what it is because it is grounded in the character of God, not in the consensus of a culture.

The responsibility before us is not to invent a new moral order. It is to remain faithful to the one that already exists.

Rebuilding begins where every lasting correction has begun — in ordinary faithfulness.

In families that choose intentional formation over passive absorption.

In churches that preach Scripture carefully rather than selectively.

In educators who value disciplined thinking over ideological conformity.

In leaders who prize integrity over expediency.

In citizens who refuse to mirror outrage and instead cultivate steadiness.

None of these actions will trend quickly. None will dominate headlines. But together, sustained across decades, they shape direction.

Cultural recalibration rarely arrives with spectacle. It unfolds gradually as communities recover coherence. It becomes visible when a generation raised within stable foundations begins to lead institutions differently. It matures when responsibility replaces reaction as the default posture.

The work is not glamorous. It is patient.

The temptation in restless ages is to chase immediacy. But durability matters more than speed. The future will not be shaped primarily by those who react most quickly, but by those who remain most consistent.

If truth is revealed, it does not require reinvention. It requires fidelity.

If dignity is bestowed by a Creator, it does not depend on affirmation to remain real.

If freedom is alignment with reality rather than escape from it, then obedience is not oppression but stability.

The cultural moment will continue to shift. New debates will replace old ones. Policies will change. Platforms will evolve. But the deeper question will remain the same: Is truth something we construct, or something we receive?

The answer to that question will determine whether fragmentation accelerates or coherence returns.

No single book will resolve that tension. No argument will settle every dispute. But lives anchored in revealed truth create communities of stability. Communities of stability influence institutions. Institutions shape culture.

The work is slow.

The work is demanding.

The work is necessary.

There may never be a public declaration that confusion has ended. There may never be universal agreement about what was lost or restored. But there will be evidence — in homes marked by clarity, in churches grounded in conviction and compassion, in leaders who value integrity over applause.

Cultural rebuilding does not require dominance. It requires endurance.

The cultural moment we inhabit did not arise overnight, and it will not recalibrate overnight. The shift toward subjective authority did not begin with a single law, court decision, or social movement. It developed through decades of philosophical assumptions gradually absorbed into education, media, and institutional life. What once appeared radical became normalized. What once felt fringe became expected.

That pattern reminds us of something important: culture is formed long before it is legislated.

If ideas shape institutions, and institutions shape imagination, then rebuilding must operate at the level of ideas first. Laws may restrain behavior. Policies may redirect systems. But only convictions produce coherence. And convictions are cultivated through formation — through teaching, example, worship, study, and disciplined reasoning.

This is why the question of authority matters so deeply. Where authority resides will determine how society understands identity, dignity, freedom, and responsibility. If authority rests in the self, then truth fluctuates with experience. If authority rests in consensus, then truth fluctuates with majority will. But if authority rests in divine revelation grounded in the created order, then truth remains steady even when human perception shifts.

A society cannot indefinitely sustain moral confidence if its foundation is unstable. When truth is continually renegotiated, exhaustion follows. When identity must be constantly asserted and defended, fragmentation intensifies. The human heart was not designed to carry the weight of self-creation.

Rebuilding, therefore, is not about nostalgia. It is about relief.

Relief from the burden of perpetual reinvention.

Relief from the anxiety of shifting moral boundaries.

Relief from the instability of competing definitions of reality.

To affirm that truth is given rather than invented is not to deny complexity. It is to anchor complexity in something enduring. It is to affirm that human dignity is not fragile because it does not depend on performance, affirmation, or self-construction. It rests in being created.

The work ahead will require humility. Those committed to revealed truth must guard against pride just as carefully as they guard against compromise. Intellectual rigor must be matched with gentleness. Conviction must be joined with patience. Cultural renewal built on arrogance collapses under its own tone.

But renewal built on coherence endures.

It is possible that this generation will not see full recalibration. History often moves slower than urgency prefers. Yet history also shows that sustained minorities shape majorities over time. Ideas planted faithfully outlive movements built on reaction.

The measure of success, then, is not immediate applause. It is fidelity.

Fidelity in families who teach patiently.

Fidelity in churches that preach clearly.

Fidelity in leaders who choose steadiness over spectacle.

Fidelity in citizens who engage without hysteria.

Such faithfulness may appear quiet. But quiet conviction has reshaped civilizations before.

The ultimate question is not whether culture is turbulent. It is whether those who believe truth is revealed will live as though it truly is.

If truth is given, it does not need reinvention.

If truth is stable, it does not require panic.

If truth is anchored in the character of God, it does not collapse when culture shifts.

Rebuilding begins when enough people believe that — and live accordingly.

And Scripture reminds us of what endurance looks like:

"Therefore, my beloved brothers, be steadfast, immovable, always abounding in the work of the Lord, knowing that in the Lord your labor is not in vain." (1 Corinthians 15:58)

Truth, unlike trend, does not expire.

It endures.

ENDNOTES

Scripture quotations are from the English Standard Version (ESV) unless otherwise noted.

1. Charles Taylor, A Secular Age (Cambridge, MA: Harvard University Press, 2007).

2. Robert N. Bellah et al., Habits of the Heart: Individualism and Commitment in American Life (Berkeley: University of California Press, 1985).

3. Robert D. Putnam, Bowling Alone: The Collapse and Revival of American Community (New York: Simon & Schuster, 2000).

4. Gallup, "U.S. Church Membership Falls Below Majority for First Time," March 29, 2021.

5. Pew Research Center, "In U.S., Decline of Christianity Continues at Rapid Pace," October 17, 2019.

6. Pew Research Center, "Americans' Trust in Government: 1958–2023."

7. Jonathan Haidt and Greg Lukianoff, The Coddling of the American Mind (New York: Penguin Press, 2018).

8. U.S. Surgeon General, "Social Media and Youth Mental Health Advisory," 2023.

9. Jonathan Haidt, The Anxious Generation (New York: Penguin Press, 2024).

10. The Cass Review, Independent Review of Gender Identity Services for Children and Young People, United Kingdom National Health Service, 2024.

11. Obergefell v. Hodges, 576 U.S. 644 (2015).

12. Bostock v. Clayton County, 590 U.S. ___ (2020).

13. Kennedy v. Bremerton School District, 597 U.S. ___ (2022).

14. U.S. Census Bureau, "Marriage and Divorce Rates," most recent annual release.

15. U.S. Census Bureau, "Living Arrangements of Children," most recent release.

16. Gallup, "Confidence in Institutions," annual survey data (most recent release).

17. Pew Research Center, "Public Trust in Government: 1958–2023."

18. Robert D. Putnam and Shaylyn Romney Garrett, The Upswing: How America Came Together a Century Ago and How We Can Do It Again (New York: Simon & Schuster, 2020).

19. Yuval Levin, A Time to Build: From Family and Community to Congress and the Campus, How Recommitting to Our Institutions Can Revive the American Dream (New York: Basic Books, 2020).

20. Mary Eberstadt, Primal Screams: How the Sexual Revolution Created Identity Politics (West Conshohocken, PA: Templeton Press, 2019).

21. Carl R. Trueman, The Rise and Triumph of the Modern Self (Wheaton, IL: Crossway, 2020).

22. Alasdair MacIntyre, After Virtue (Notre Dame, IN: University of Notre Dame Press, 1981).

23. Philip Rieff, The Triumph of the Therapeutic (Chicago: University of Chicago Press, 1966).

24. Sherry Turkle, Alone Together: Why We Expect More from Technology and Less from Each Other (New York: Basic Books, 2011).

25. Jean M. Twenge, iGen (New York: Atria Books, 2017).

26. Pew Research Center, "Modeling the Future of Religion in America," September 13, 2022.

27. Gallup, "U.S. Church Membership Falls Below Majority for First Time," March 29, 2021. (If already cited earlier, you may consolidate numbering as needed.)

28. United Methodist Church, "Protocol of Reconciliation & Grace Through Separation" (2020) and related General Conference materials.

29. Global Methodist Church, "Statement of Doctrines and Discipline," 2022.

30. Lifeway Research, "Pastors' Views on Cultural Issues," most recent survey release.

31. Brookings Institution, "Declining Trust in Institutions in the United States," most recent report.

32. American Enterprise Institute (AEI), Survey Center on American Life, "Survey on Community and Social Trust," most recent release.

33. National Center for Education Statistics (NCES), "Digest of Education Statistics," most recent release.

34. Jonathan Rauch, The Constitution of Knowledge: A Defense of Truth (Washington, DC: Brookings Institution Press, 2021).

35. U.S. Surgeon General, "Our Epidemic of Loneliness and Isolation," 2023 Advisory.

36. Robert Nisbet, The Quest for Community (New York: Oxford University Press, 1953).

37. National Institutes of Health (NIH), studies on social isolation and health outcomes, most recent summaries.

38. Pew Research Center, "Teens, Social Media and Technology," most recent release.

39. James Davison Hunter, To Change the World (New York: Oxford University Press, 2010).

40. Timothy Keller, Center Church (Grand Rapids: Zondervan, 2012). (Optional but helpful for pastoral rebuilding framework.)

CONTINUE THE CONVERSATION

If *It's Not My Truth, It's the Truth* challenged you, encouraged you, or helped you think more clearly about truth in a culture of confusion, I invite you to continue the conversation.

The issues facing our culture today are not small, and they will not be solved by silence. They require people who are willing to stand firmly for what is true.

Faith Vanguard exists to encourage that kind of courage.

Scan the QR code below to:

- Read new articles and insights

- Stay informed on future books and resources

- Follow the ongoing work of Faith Vanguard

Stand firm. Speak boldly.

https://www.faithvanguard.org

A SMALL FAVOR

Thank you for reading *It's Not My Truth, It's the Truth.*

If this book challenged you, encouraged you, or helped clarify the importance of truth in today's culture, would you consider taking a moment to leave a short review?

Your review helps more readers discover the book and join the conversation about truth in a culture increasingly shaped by relativism.

Reviews do not need to be long—even a few sentences can make a difference.

Thank you for your support.

— Scott Farley

ALSO BY SCOTT FARLEY

Faith Vanguard: The Urgent Call To Awaken America